The Hampstead Clinic Psychoanalytic Library
(Concept Research Group)

VOLUME II

BASIC PSYCHOANALYTIC CONCEPTS ON THE THEORY OF DREAMS

BASIC PSYCHOANALYTIC CONCEPTS ON THE THEORY OF DREAMS

by

HUMBERTO NAGERA

and

S. BAKER, A. COLONNA, R. EDGCUMBE,
A. HOLDER, L. KEARNEY, M. KAWENOKA,
C. LEGG, D. MEERS, L. NEURATH, K. REES

MARESFIELD REPRINTS
LONDON

First published in 1969.
Reprinted 1981, with permission
of George Allen & Unwin, Ltd. by
H. Karnac (Books) Limited
56-58 Gloucester Road
London, S.W. 7, England

ISBN 0 9507146 4 X

MANUFACTURED IN THE UNITED STATES OF AMERICA

ACKNOWLEDGEMENTS AND COPYRIGHT NOTICES

The editor and publishers wish to thank the following publishers for their kind permission to use the material noted:

The Hogarth Press and the London Institute of Psychoanalysis for permission to quote from all volumes of the Standard Edition of the Complete Psychological Works of Sigmund Freud.

W. W. Norton for permission to quote from the following publications of Freud:
On Dreams
Jokes and their Relation to the Unconscious
The Psychopathology of Everyday Life
An Outline of Psychoanalysis
An Autobiographical Study
New Introductory Lectures on Psycho-analysis.

Liveright for permission to quote from the following publications of Freud:
Beyond The Pleasure Principle
Introductory Lectures on Psychoanalysis.
Thanks are due to the *Sigmund Freud Copyrights* for their permission and generous co-operation.

FOREWORD TO
THE HAMPSTEAD CLINIC LIBRARY

The series of publications of which the present volume forms a part, will be welcomed by all those readers who are concerned with the history of psychoanalytic concepts and interested to follow the vicissitudes of their fate through the theoretical, clinical and technical writings of psychoanalytic authors. On the one hand, these fates may strike us as being very different from each other. On the other hand, it proves not too difficult to single out some common trends and to explore the reasons for them.

There are some terms and concepts which served an important function for psychoanalysis in its earliest years because of their being simple and all-embracing such as for example the notion of a *complex*. Even the lay public understood more or less easily that what was meant thereby was any cluster of impulses, emotions, thoughts, etc. which have their roots in the unconscious and, exerting their influence from there, give rise to anxiety, defences and symptom formation in the conscious mind. Accordingly, the term was used widely as a form of psychological short-hand. 'Father-Complex', 'Mother-Complex', 'Guilt-Complex', 'Inferiority-Complex', etc., became familiar notions. Nevertheless, in due course, added psycho-analytical findings about the child's relationship to his parents, about the early mother-infant tie and its consequences, about the complexities of lacking self-esteem and feelings of insufficiency and inferiority demanded more precise conceptualization. The very omnibus nature of the term could not but lead to its, at least partial, abandonment. All that remained from it were the terms 'Oedipus-Complex' to designate the experiences centred around the triangular relationships of the phallic phase, and 'Castration-Complex' for the anxieties, repressed wishes, etc., concerning the loss or lack of the male sexual organ.

If, in the former instance, a general concept was split up to make room for more specific meanings, in other instances concepts took turns in the opposite direction. After starting out as concrete, well-defined descriptions of circumscribed psychic events, they were applied by many authors to an ever-widening circle of phenomena until their connotation became increasingly vague and imprecise and until finally special efforts had to be made to re-define them, to restrict their sphere of application and to invest them once more with precision and significance. This is what happened, for example, to the concepts of 'Transference' and of 'Trauma'.

The concept and term 'transference' was designed originally to establish the fact that the realistic relationship between analyst and patient is invariably distorted by fantasies and object-relations which stem from the patient's past and that these very distortions can be turned into a technical tool to reveal the patient's past pathogenic history. In present days, the meaning of the term has been widened to the extent that it comprises whatever happens between analyst and patient regardless of its derivation and of the reasons for its happening.

A 'trauma' or 'traumatic happening' meant originally an (external or internal) event of a magnitude with which the individual's ego is unable to deal, i.e. a sudden influx of excitation, massive enough to break through the ego's normal stimulus barrier. To this purely quantitative meaning of the term were added in time all sorts of qualifications (such as cumulative, retrospective, silent, beneficial), until the concept ended up as more or less synonymous with the notion of a pathogenic event in general.

Psychoanalytic concepts may be overtaken also by a further fate, which is perhaps of even greater significance. Most of them owe their origin to a particular era of psychoanalytic theory, or to a particular field of clinical application, or to a particular mode of technique. Since any of the backgrounds in which they are rooted, are open to change, this should lead either to a corresponding change in the concepts or to their abandonment. But, most frequently, this has failed to happen. Many concepts are carried forward through the changing scene of psychoanalytic theory and practice without sufficient thought being given to their necessary alteration or re-definition.

A case in kind is the concept of 'acting out'. It was created at the very outset of technical thinking and teaching, tied to the treatment of neurotic patients, and it characterized originally a specific reaction of these patients to the psychoanalytic technique, namely that certain items of their past, when retrieved from the unconscious, did not return to conscious memory but revealed themselves instead in behaviour, were 'acted on', or 'acted out' instead of being remembered. By now, this clear distinction between remembering the recovered past and re-living it has been obscured; the term 'acting out' is used out of this context, notably for patients such as adolescents, delinquents or psychotics whose impulse-ridden behaviour is part of their original pathology and not the direct consequence of analytic work done on the ego's defences against the repressed unconscious.

It was in this state of affairs that *Dr H. Nagera* initiated his enquiry into the history of psychoanalytic thinking. Assisted by a team of analytic workers, trained in the Hampstead Child-Therapy Course and Clinic, he set out to trace the course of basic psychoanalytic concepts from their first appearance through their changes in the twenty-three Volumes of the Standard Edition of the Complete Psychological Works of Sigmund Freud, i.e. to a point from where they are meant to be taken further to include the writings of the most important authors of the post-Freudian era.

Dr Nagera's aim in this venture was a fourfold one:

to facilitate for readers of psychoanalytic literature the understanding of psychoanalytic thought and of the terminology in which it is expressed;

to understand and define concepts, not only according to their individual significance, but also according to their relevance for the particular historical phase of psychoanalytic theory within which they have arisen;

to induce psychoanalytic authors to use their terms and concepts more precisely with regard for the theoretical framework to which they owe their origin, and to reduce thereby the many sources of misunderstanding and confusion which govern the psychoanalytic literature at present;

finally, to create for students of psychoanalysis the opportunity to embark on a course of independent reading and study, linked to a scholarly aim and designed to promote their critical and constructive thinking on matters of theory-formation.

Anna Freud, London, August 1968

CONTENTS

INTRODUCTION

This volume is a sample of scholastic research work carried out at the Hampstead Child-Therapy Course and Clinic relating to the study of a large number of pre-selected basic psychoanalytic concepts postulated and developed by Freud in his psychoanalytic writings, spanning the time from his earliest to his latest conceptualizations.

This research work has been carried out during the last six years by the Concept Research Group. These drafts on basic concepts are in no way meant to replace the study of Freud's works themselves. On the contrary, they are intended as a guide to help the student in that very aim.

The group's method has been to assign to each of its members one pre-selected concept at a time. This member's task then is to extract all the relevant material from Freud's published papers, books, correspondence, Minutes of the Meetings of the Vienna Psychoanalytic Society, etc., and to prepare a written summary of a given concept for discussion. This first draft is referred to as the 'personal draft' and is circulated among members some time before it is due for discussion.

As far as possible the draft makes use of 'literal quotations', giving at the same time the source of the quotations. This facilitates the study of the drafts by the group members who meet weekly to discuss the personal drafts. On the basis of the general discussion by the Group a second draft is produced which we designate as the 'group draft'.

Our aims are multiple and are very much in accordance with the views expressed by Hartmann, Kris and Loewenstein in their paper 'The Function of Theory in Psychoanalysis'[1] and in other publications.

Like these authors, we believe that Freud's views are often misrepresented in a considerable number of the vast amount of

[1] Hartmann, H., Kris, E., Loewenstein, R. M., 'The Function of Theory in Psychoanalysis', *Drives, Affects and Behaviour*, International Universities Press, Inc., New York, 1953.

psychoanalytic writings due to the fact that certain of Freud's statements are not always evaluated within their proper context. Thus, not infrequently, specific aspects are torn out of a long historical line of theoretical development and isolated from the rest, and similarly one or the other phase of psychoanalytic thinking is given undue emphasis out of context. Such misrepresentations are apt to convey the erroneous impression that whatever aspect has been singled out embraces all that Freud or psychoanalysis had ever to say on some specific topic. In this sense we very much endorse the statement made by Hartmann, Kris and Loewenstein that 'quoting Freud is, as a rule, meaningful only if it is part of a laborious but unavoidable attempt to gain insight into the position of the quoted passage within the development of Freud's thought'.[1] This is precisely one of the major aims of the Concept Research Group.

We were similarly prompted for what we felt with Hartmann, Kris and Loewenstein, to be 'the disregard for the psychoanalytic theory as a coherent set of assumptions'.[2] Freud's hypotheses are interrelated in a systematic way: there is a hierarchy of hypothesis in their relevance, their closeness to observation, their degree of verification. It is none the less true that there exists no comprehensive presentation of analysis from this angle. Here again recourse to the historical approach seems imperative . . . by showing the actual problems in their right proportions and in their right perspective.'[3]

Another important factor is the realization that Freud made many statements in the course of developing his theories which he withdrew or modified in subsequent works. This in itself constitutes a major source of frequent misrepresentation of Freud's views. One of the aims of this work, in which we try to evaluate Freud's basic psychoanalytic concepts in their historical context, is precisely to avoid such pitfalls and misrepresentations.

We further agree with Hartmann, Kris and Loewenstein that a

---

[1] Hartmann, H., 'The Development of the Ego Concept in Freud's Work', I.J.P., Vol. XXXVII, Part VI, 1956. (Paper read at the Freud Centenary Meeting of the British Psycho-Analytical Society, May 5, 1956.)

[2] Hartmann, H., Kris, E., Loewenstein, R. M., 'The Function of Theory in Psychoanalysis', *Drives, Affects and Behaviour*, International Universities Press, Inc., New York, 1953, p. 23.

[3] Hartmann, H., 'The Development of the Ego Concept in Freud's Work', I.J.P., Vol. XXXVII, Part VI, London 1956, p. 425.

serious danger of misrepresentation exists when there is an insufficient understanding of the hierarchy of psychoanalytic propositions. It is therefore essential to have a clear understanding of how the different parts of psychoanalytic theoretical propositions fit together, both when quoting and when attempting new formulations.

We are planning to publish the remainder of the work of the Concept Research Group up to the present moment in the near future in order to make it available to teachers and students in the psychoanalytic and related fields. We think that this contribution will be of special value and interest to any student of Freud, especially students in training who will have an encyclopaedic review of basic psychoanalytic concepts in an extremely condensed but meaningful way. From these summaries of concepts the student can readily find his way back to Freud's work in order to pursue and become more fully acquainted with his formulations. In this way he can study specific aspects in the development of the theory while being able, at the same time, to get a more comprehensive and over-all view of the particular topic and its relations with other aspects of the theory. We believe that our work will be similarly useful to lecturers and seminar leaders, to research workers in the field of psychoanalysis and related fields and to those writing papers which require a review of Freud's statements with regard to a specific topic. Altogether this form of scholastic research may help to avoid confusion, constant reformulations and the introduction of new terms when authors in fact refer to 'concepts' already clearly described by Freud in the past. This work may well help to open the way to standardize and find some measure of agreement as to the precise meaning of terms used in psychoanalysis today.

Although we have taken as much care as possible to be comprehensive and to avoid misrepresentations, experience has taught us that we can have no claim to perfection or completeness. It is practically impossible, within a vast and complex volume of theory such as Freud's life output represents, not to overlook or even slightly to misrepresent one or another aspect or set of factors. Furthermore, the capacity to comprehend and the level of insight possible for any given person or group of persons engaged in such work increases as the work proceeds. Thus certain formulations become more meaningful, are suddenly understood in a new light, assume a different significance, etc. Because of our realization of potential shortcomings we hope that future readers of these concepts will contribute to complete and clarify the work which the Concept Group has started, by drawing our attention to relevant material which has been either overlooked, misrepresented or not understood in its full significance.

It is hoped that in this way the Concepts will become more and more representative and complete in the course of time.

DR HUMBERTO NAGERA.

THE CONCEPT OF DREAMS

Definition of Dreams

A dream is the (disguised) fulfilment of a (repressed) wish.[1] This formulation may be regarded as Freud's most concise definition of a dream. A comprehensive definition of dreams, as conceived by Freud, should cover the total phenomenon of which the latent dream content, the dream-work and the manifest dream are the several, component parts. The dream-work is the most 'essential' part.[2] Only through understanding its laws and conditions can we reach the latent dream content which contains the true and disguised wish.[3]

Dreams are the fulfilment of wishes[4] in the service of the preservation of sleep. This was later qualified by the statement that dreams are the 'attempted' fulfilment of wishes.[5] 'We have accepted the idea that the reason why dreams are invariably wish-fulfilments is that they are products of the system Unconscious, whose activity knows no other aim than the fulfilment of wishes and which has at its command no other forces than wishful impulses'.[6] It is for this reason that Freud wrote that *the interpretation of dreams is the royal road to a knowledge of the unconscious activities of the mind*.[7] A dream is also described as a *substitute for an infantile scene modified by being transferred on to a recent experience*,[8] and as the expression of *a piece of infantile mental life that has been superseded*.[9]

[1] (1900a) *The Interpretation of Dreams*, The Standard Edition of the Complete Psychological Works of Sigmund Freud (hereafter referred to as S.E.), Vol. 4, p. 160; (cf. also (1901a) *On Dreams*, S.E., Vol. 15, p. 674 and (1925d) *An Autobiographical Study*, S.E., Vol. 20, p. 45).
[2] (1933a) *New Introductory Lectures on Psycho-Analysis*, S.E., Vol. 22, p. 8.
[3] (1900a) *The Interpretation of Dreams*, S.E., Vol. 4, p. 134.
[4] (1916–17) *Introductory Lectures on Psycho-Analysis*, S.E., Vol. 15–16, pp. 128–9.
[5] (1933a) *New Introductory Lectures on Psycho-Analysis*, S.E., Vol. 22, p. 28.
[6] (1900a) *The Interpretation of Dreams*, S.E., Vol. 5, p. 568; (1933a) *New Introductory Lectures on Psycho-Analysis*, S.E., Vol. 22, p. 18.
[7] (1900a) *The Interpretation of Dreams*, S.E., Vol. 5, p. 608.
[8] ibid, S.E., Vol. 5, p. 546.
[9] ibid, S.E., Vol. 5, p. 567.

Though Freud referred to dreams as transient psychoses[1] neurotic symptoms in themselves[2] and considered them to be similar to the same set of psycho-pathological structures as *idées fixes*, obsessions and delusions,[3] there is no doubt that he did not consider dreams as pathological phenomena in themselves. 'Dreams are not pathological phenomena; they can appear in any healthy person under the conditions of a state of sleep'.[4] The link with the psychoses prompts itself by the common element of the hallucinatory wish-fulfilment,[5] that (the link) with a neurotic symptom by the dream's characteristic of being 'a compromise between the demands of a repressed impulse and the resistance of a censoring force in the ego'.[6]

Freud's conceptualization of dreams must be seen in contrast to earlier and current medical theories about dreams. Referring to these he wrote that:

'To concern oneself with dreams is not merely unpractical and uncalled-for, it is positively disgraceful. It brings with it the odium of being unscientific and rouses the suspicion of a personal inclination to mysticism. . . . We may therefore ask what may be the true source of the contempt in which dreams are held in scientific circles. It is, I believe, a reaction against the overvaluation of dreams in earlier days . . . interest in dreams sank to the level of superstition. . . . On the other hand the exact science of today has repeatedly concerned itself with dreams but always with the sole aim of applying its physiological theories to them. Medical men, of course, looked on dreams as non-psychical acts, as the expression in mental life of somatic stimuli. . . . Can you imagine what exact science would say if it learnt that we want to make an attempt to discover the *sense* of dreams? Perhaps it has already said it. But we will not let ourselves be frightened off. If it was possible for parapraxes to have a sense, dreams can have one too; and in a great many cases parapraxes have a sense, which has

[1] (1916b) 'A Mythological Parallel to a Visual Obsession', S.E., Vol. 14, p. 230.
[2] (1916–17) *Introductory Lectures on Psycho-Analysis*, S.E., Vol. 15–16, p. 83. (1925d) *An Autobiographical Study*, S.E., Vol. 20, p. 45.
[3] (1900a) *The Interpretation of Dreams*, S.E., Vol. 4, p. 281.
[4] (1916–17) *Introductory Lectures on Psycho-Analysis*, S.E., Vol. 16, p. 297.
[5] (1916b) 'A Mythological Parallel to a Visual Obsession', S.E., Vol. 14, pp. 229–31.
[6] (1925d) *An Autobiographical Study*, S.E., Vol. 20, p. 45.

escaped exact science. So let us embrace the prejudice of the ancients and of the people and let us follow in the footsteps of the dream interpreters of antiquity'.[1]

From this point of view the following characteristics and functions must be emphasized as particularly relevant:

1. *Dreams are a product of the mind*
Dreams are 'not merely a somatic process . . . they are not meaningless . . . they are not absurd . . . they are psychical phenomena of complete validity—fulfilments of wishes: they can be inserted into the chain of intelligible waking mental acts; they are constructed by a highly complicated activity of the mind',[2] in spite of the fact that the finished product strikes us as something alien.[3] Two essential features of dream-life contribute to this latter impression, namely 'the incapacity for ideational work of the kind which we feel as intentionally willed' and the emergence of visual images.[4] Freud also calls dreaming 'another kind of remembering though one that is subject to the conditions that rule at night and to the laws of dream-formation'.[5] Dreams 'are a residue of mental activity, made possible by the fact that the narcissistic state of sleep has not been able to be completely established'.[6] 'A dream, then, is the manner in which the mind reacts to stimuli that impinge upon it in the state of sleep.'[7]

2. *Dreams are a form of thinking*
'Dreams are nothing other than a particular *form* of thinking, made possible by the conditions of the state of sleep'[8] and created by the dream work. 'A dream is not the "unconscious"; it is the form into which a thought over from preconscious, or even from conscious, waking life, can, thanks to the favouring state of sleep, be recast.

[1] (1916–17) *Introductory Lectures on Psycho-Analysis*, S.E., Vol. 15–16, pp. 84–7.

[2] (1900a) *The Interpretation of Dreams*, S.E., Vol. 4, p. 122.

[3] ibid, p. 48, p. 122 (cf. also (1916–17) *Introductory Lectures on Psycho-Analysis*, S.E., Vol. 15–16, p. 88).

[4] ibid, p. 48. (1916–17) *Introductory Lectures on Psycho-Analysis*, S.E., Vol. 15–16, p. 90.

[5] (1918b) 'From the History of an Infantile Neurosis', S.E., Vol. 17, p. 51.

[6] (1917d) 'A Metapsychological Supplement to the Theory of Dreams', S.E., Vol. 14, p. 234.

[7] (1916–17) *Introductory Lectures on Psycho-Analysis*, S.E., Vol. 15, p. 89.

[8] [1925] (1900a) *The Interpretation of Dreams*, S.E., Vol. 5, pp. 506–7f.

In the state of sleep this thought has been reinforced by un-conscious wishful impulses and has thus experienced distortion through the dream work, which is determined by the mechanisms prevailing in the unconscious'.[1]

It is a particular form of thinking in which 'we appear not to *think* but to *experience*; that is to say, we attach complete belief to the hallucinations'.[2]

3. *Dreams preserve sleep*
'*Dreams are the GUARDIANS of sleep and not its disturbers*'.[2]
'Dreams are things which get rid of (psychical stimuli disturbing the sleep, by the method of hallucinatory satisfaction'.[3]

4. *A Dream is a compromise-formation*
'The dream is already a compromise-structure. It has a double function; on the one hand it is ego-syntonic, since, by getting rid of the stimuli which are interfering with sleep, it serves the wish to sleep; on the other hand it allows a repressed instinctual impulse to obtain the satisfaction that is possible in these circumstances, in the form of the hallucinated fulfilment of a wish'.[4]

---

[1] (1920a) 'A Case of Homosexuality in a Woman', S.E., Vol. 18, pp. 165–6.
[2] (1900a) *The Interpretation of Dreams*, S.E., Vol. 4–5, p. 50.
[3] ibid, pp. 123, 227, 233, 554.
[4] (1916–17) *Introductory Lectures on Psycho-Analysis*, S.E., Vol. 15, p. 136.

DREAM SOURCES

Dream Instigators

Freud speaks at different points of 'instigating sources', or 'instigators', or 'sources' using these terms synonymously. It is nevertheless sometimes implicit that these are concepts of a somewhat different nature. 'Dream sources' mainly relates to the sources from which the material to build the dream is taken (in the sense of content), while 'dream instigators' is more in the nature of an energic concept describing 'foci' of energy that has remained or becomes active during sleep, thus threatening the ego wish to sleep. Sometimes these two factors are combined with preconscious thoughts or ideas that refuse to obey the ego wish to sleep and can not be wholly emptied of their cathexis. Thus they are at the same time a 'source' of content for the dream (the thought or the idea as such) and a 'foci' of energy (the cathexis that remains attached to the thought). Clearly, much of the material used in any given dream did not 'instigate' the dream.

The term 'source' has on the other hand the connotation of 'origin' and in this respect the 'source' of dreams contents can be best described with reference to the repressed unconscious, the mnemic systems and the preconscious system. These aspects are covered in detail in the Concepts dealing with Day Residues, Latent Dream-Thoughts, Dream Wishes, etc.

'Most authorities seem to agree in assuming that the causes that disturb sleep—that is, the sources of dreaming—may be of many kinds and that somatic stimuli and mental excitations alike may come to act as instigators of dreams. Opinions differ widely, however, in the preference they show for one or the other sources of dreams and in the order of importance which they assign to them as factors in the production of dreams'.[1] In finally comparing his conclusions with those of previous and contemporary scientists, Freud states that in his theory of dreams and dreaming based on interpretation, he has found room for most of their contradictory

[1] (1900a) *The Interpretation of Dreams*, S.E., Vol. 4, p. 22.

views but the one that claims that dreams are meaningless processes, and the one stating that dreaming is a purely somatic
process.[1] Wherever he has to reject completely a source adduced
by other authors, e.g., subjective states of excitation in sense
organs during sleep, he could explain them on psychical grounds.
The result is a re-evaluation of previous assumed dream-source
and the addition of the most essential sources of motivating power
which make dreaming into a highly meaningful and purposive
psychical activity in the state of sleep.[2]

'Any complete enumeration of the sources of dreams leads to a
recognition of four kinds of source; and these have also been used
for the classification of dreams themselves. They are: (1) external
(objective) sensory excitations; (2) internal (subjective) sensory
excitations; (3) internal (organic) somatic stimuli; and (4) purely
psychical sources of stimulation'.[3] As regards point (2) in this
classification, viz. the internal (subjective) sensory excitations,
Freud holds that there is no need to assume a state of internal
excitation—impossible to prove objectively—but that the state of
excitation has been set up by a revived memory, e.g. of a visual
excitation, which was originally an immediate one.[4]

In chapter V of *The Interpretation of Dreams*, Freud goes on to
examine the source from which the material of dreams is taken.
The sources of the material of dreams he describes as:

(A) Recent and Indifferent Material in Dreams.
(B) Infantile Material as a Source of Dreams.
(C) The Somatic Sources of Dreams.

(For the categories A and B the reader should consult '*Day's
Residues*', '*Latent Dream Thoughts*', '*Affects*', etc.).

It is important to note that Freud considers that while material
from all sources can form part of the content of a dream the
motivating power is always an infantile repressed wish, impulse or
experience, and is the true and ultimate source of motivating
power for the formation of a dream.[5] (See 'Latent Dream Content,'
'Dream Wishes'.)

---

[1] (1900a) *The Interpretation of Dreams*, S.E., Vol. 5, p. 588.
[2] ibid, pp. 589–92.
[3] (1900a) *The Interpretation of Dreams*, S.E., Vol. 4, p. 22.
[4] (1900a) *The Interpretation of Dreams*, S.E., Vol. 5, pp. 546 and 589.
[5] (1900a) *The Interpretation of Dreams*, S.E., Vol. 4–5, pp. 86 f., 191, 193,
204 f., 553, 561 (cf. also (1925d [1924]) *An Autobiographical Study*, S.E., Vol.
20, p. 44).

As for (C), the somatic sources of dreams, Freud has pointed out how the source of some material in the manifest dream content can be found in somatic stimuli during sleep, but not as often as it used to be thought and not usually as an exclusive source. Since, in Freud's definition, a dream is a reaction to 'everything that is simultaneously present in the sleeping mind as currently active material',[1] somatic stimuli act as additional sources to the psychical ones[2] and, together with the *Day's Residues*, are worked up into a wish fulfilment.[3] Such stimuli may be external or internal perceptions, i.e. stimuli such as auditory, tactile, pain, hunger, thirst, sexual. Such external or internal nervous stimuli, if intense enough to arouse psychical awareness in sleep, serve as a nodal point for the formation of a dream while a wish, not necessarily a currently active one, has to supply reinforcing energy, both acting together as instigating sources. Unpleasureable sensations arising from somatic sources during sleep may also serve for the disguised fulfilment of a repressed wish.[4]

Only occasionally, if very strong and if very threatening to the maintenance of the sleeping state, can internal somatic stimuli act as effective instigators of a dream without a link with psychically significant sources. Such dreams of 'convenience' may show in their manifest content the need or wish as fulfilled either openly or under a transparent symbolic disguise.[5] This applies particularly to dreams of young children.[6] In adults such dreams usually do not for long succeed in maintaining sleep.[7]

On the whole Freud holds that, in view of the variety of possible dream responses to somatic source of stimulation,[8] such sources play a similar part as instigating sources as recent but indifferent preconscious day's residues: they are used if they fit in with the psychically significant instigating sources.[9] In general, elements in

[1] ibid., Vol. 4, pp. 179, 229.
[2] ibid., p. 228 f.
[3] (1933a) *New Introductory Lectures on Psycho-Analysis*, S.E., Vol. 22, p. 31 (cf. also (1940a /1938]) *An Outline of Psycho-Analysis*, S.E., Vol. 23, pp. 88, 92).
[4] ibid., pp. 236, 256, 267.
[5] ibid., pp. 316, 396, 402 f. footnote.
[6] ibid., Vol. 5, pp. 644–6 (cf. also (1925d [1924]), *An Autobiographical Study*, S.E., Vol. 20, p. 46).
[7] ibid., Vol. 4, p. 402.
[8] ibid., pp. 224–7.
[9] ibid., p. 237 f. (cf. also (1907a), *Delusions and Dreams in Jensen's Gradiva*, S.E., Vol. 9, p. 56).

the manifest dream which are derivatives of sensory stimuli during sleep are not more vivid than those derived from memories.

In dreams, incipient physical disease can often be detected earlier than in waking life; all the current bodily sensations assume gigantic proportions (a magnification which is hypochondriacal in character owing to the narcissistic state of sleep). This diagnostic value of such dreams is generally recognized.[1] Somatically determined feelings of anxiety during sleep may appear in the manifest dream content where they refer to an insufficiently disguised deeply repressed wish.[2] (See *Anxiety Dreams*.)

In 1938[3] Freud reformulated his theory in structural terms; dream-instigating sources can be either an id impulse (an unconscious wish either repressed or arising from a current somatic excitation) obtruding into the ego, or a preconscious conflicting chain of thoughts, an ego-desire (day's residue) which is reinforced by an unconscious element. In both cases the demand is made upon the sleeping ego which, intent on its wish to maintain sleep, attempts to get rid of the disturbing demands by the formation of a dream which, in disguised and distorted shape in its manifest content, fulfills the wish.

[1] ibid., p. 72 (cf. also 'A Metaptychological Supplement to the Theory of Dreams', S.E., Vol. 14, p. 223).

[2] ibid., pp. 34, 236, 267.

[3] (1940a [1938]) *An Outline of Psycho-Analysis*, S.E., Vol. 23, pp. 27, 31–3.

THE DREAM-WISH

Freud speaks of 'the dream-wish' in one of two ways: (a) to refer specifically to a wish originating from the unconscious, (b) to refer to a compromise wish constructed from the unconscious wish and the preconscious dream thoughts by the dream work. (See 'The Dream-Work'.) Dreams, or the process of dreaming, may fulfil a number of other wishes as well. (See 'Other Wishes in Dreams and Dreaming'.) But only the unconscious wish is the indispensable element in the formation of the dream wish.

In *The Interpretation of Dreams* Freud laid particular emphasis on the role of the unconscious wish, and used the term 'dream wish' mainly in the first sense given above. He said that the motive force for the construction of a dream is invariably a wish or wishes from the unconscious.[1]

'... the reason why dreams are invariably wish-fulfilments is that they are products of the system unconscious, whose activity knows no other aim than the fulfilment of wishes and which has at its command no other forces than wishful impulses.'[2]

Freud discussed four apparently possible origins for the wishes that come true in dreams, namely, (a) wishes aroused during the day but left unfulfilled, which remain in the preconscious; (b) wishes which arose during the day but were repudiated and repressed, i.e. driven out of the preconscious into the unconscious; (c) wishes belonging to the unconscious and incapable of passing beyond it; (d) wishes arising during the night stimulated by bodily needs. He went on to emphasize, however, that though categories a, b and d might contribute to the instigation of a dream, the dream cannot be formed without the wish from the unconscious.[3]

'*My supposition is that a conscious wish can only become a dream-instigator if it succeeds in awakening an unconscious wish with the*

---

[1] (1900a) *The Interpretation of Dreams*, S.E., Vol. 5, p. 560 f.
[2] Ibid., p. 568.
[3] ibid., pp. 551–3.

THE THEORY OF DREAMS

same tenor and in obtaining reinforcement from it. From indications derived from the psychoanalysis of the neuroses, I consider that these unconscious wishes are always on the alert, ready at any time to find their way to expression when an opportunity arises for allying themselves with an impulse from the conscious and for transferring their own great intensity on to the latter's lesser one. It will then *appear* as though the conscious wish alone had been realized in the dream; only some small peculiarity in the dream's configuration will serve as a finger-post to put us on the track of the powerful ally from the unconscious. . . . But these wishes, held under repression, are themselves of infantile origin, as we are taught by psychological research into the neuroses. I would propose, therefore, to set aside the assertion made just now, that the place of origin of dream-wishes is a matter of indifference and replace it by another one to the following effect: *a wish which is represented in a dream must be an infantile one*. In the case of adults it originates from the *unconscious*, in the case of children, where there is as yet no division or censorship between the preconscious and the unconscious, or where that division is only gradually being set up, it is an unfulfilled, unrepressed wish from waking life. I am aware that this assertion cannot be proved to hold universally; but it can be proved to hold frequently, even in unsuspected cases, and it cannot be *contradicted* as a general proposition.'[1]

In *The Interpretation of Dreams* Freud discussed the importance of the day's residues, not only conscious wishes but ideas and indifferent or insignificant impressions.[2] They are essential ingredients in dreams because unconscious wishes are quite incapable of entering the preconscious, and so must establish a connection with a preconscious idea onto which they can transfer their intensity.[3] These recent and indifferent elements are much more likely to escape censorship than the unconscious wish.[4]

'It will be seen, then, that the day's residues, among which we may now class the indifferent impressions, not only *borrow* something from the *unconscious* when they succeed in taking a share in the formation of a dream—namely the instinctual force which

---

[1] ibid., p. 553 f.
[2] ibid., pp. 562–4.
[3] ibid., p. 562.
[4] ibid., p. 563.

is at the disposal of the repressed wish—but that they also *offer* the unconscious something indispensable—namely the necessary point of attachment for a transference.'[1]

In 'A Metapsychological Supplement to the Theory of Dreams' Freud used the term 'dream-wish' mainly in the second sense noted above: that of a compromise formation. In this paper he discussed the process of dream-formation, and the interaction between the day's residues and the unconscious wish. In sleep the systems unconscious and preconscious are not entirely emptied of cathexis even though the wish to sleep requires a complete withdrawal of cathexis, because the unconscious resists this demand.[2] He describes the first two phases in dream-formation.

'The resistance of the day's residues may originate in a link with unconscious impulses which is already in existence during waking life; or the process may be somewhat less simple, and the day's residues which have not been wholly emptied of cathexis may establish a connection with the repressed material only after the state of sleep has set in, thanks to the easing of communication between the preconscious and unconscious. In both cases there follows the same decisive step in dream-formation. The preconscious dream-wish is formed, which *gives expression to the unconscious impulse in the material of the preconscious day's residues.* This dream-wish must be sharply distinguished from the day's residues; it need not have existed in waking life and it may already display the irrational character possessed by everything that is unconscious when we translate it into the conscious. Again, the dream-wish must not be confused with the wishful impulses which may have been present, though they certainly need not necessarily be present, amongst the preconscious (latent) dream-thoughts. If, however, there *were* any such preconscious wishes, the dream-wish associates itself with them, as a most effective reinforcement of them.'[3]

The Third phase in dream-formation is the regression to perception.[4] 'The dream-wish, as we say, is *hallucinated*, and, as a hallucination, meets with belief in the reality of its fulfilment.[5]

[1] ibid., p. 564.
[2] (1917d [1915]) 'A Metapsychological Supplement to the Theory of Dreams' S.E., Vol. 14, p. 225.
[3] ibid., p. 226.   [4] ibid., pp. 227–9.   [5] ibid., p. 229.

OTHER WISHES IN DREAMS AND DREAMING

1. *The Wish to Sleep*
Dreaming is a process which serves the wish to sleep by dealing with disturbing psychical and sensory stimuli in such a way as to permit sleep to continue. '*Dreams are the Guardians of sleep and not its disturbers*'.[1] In topographical terminology the wish to sleep belongs to the preconscious,[2] structurally it belongs to the ego.[3] Sleep may be disturbed by internal or external sensory stimuli, by pre-occupations, anxieties and preconscious wishes left over from waking life, as well as by unconscious wishes that press towards consciousness.[4] By linking preconscious psychic excitations and somatic excitations with an unconscious wish, and working them up into a dream-wish which is presented as fulfilled in the dream, the dream work permits sleep to continue. If, however, the dream work fails satisfactorily to deal with these disturbing excitations, the dreamer awakens.[5, 6]

2. Within the dream itself other wishes may be expressed with varying degrees of disguise, or may be used in the construction of the manifest dream, besides the unconscious wish which is the indispensable element in the formation of the main dream-wish.

(*a*) Preconscious wishes left over from waking life may be used in the dream but only if they can link up with an unconscious wish. As a result of the dream work it may appear as if a preconscious wish is the only one expressed in the dream. These preconscious wishes may be wishes that occurred but were repudiated

---

[1] (1900a) *The Interpretation of Dreams*, S.E., Vol. 4, p. 233 f.
[2] ibid., S.E., Vol. 5, p. 570.
[3] (1933a) *New Introductory Lectures on Psycho-Analysis*, S.E., Vol. 22, p. 19.
[4] (1900a) *The Interpretation of Dreams*, S.E., Vols. 4 and 5, pp. 123–5, 22 7f., 233–5, 554.
[5] ibid., pp. 577–9.
[6] (1901a) *On Dreams*, S.E., Vol. 5, pp. 678–81.

26

and repressed during waking life, or they may have been left unfulfilled without undergoing repression.[1]

(b) Censorship or Superego wishes may be expressed in unpleasant dreams, e.g. punishment dreams. Where this occurs the superego wish is not, however, the only wish expressed in the latent dream content. There is, as usual, the dream wish, but this has not been sufficiently disguised to evade the censorship. There arises, therefore, the wish that the dreamer may be punished for repressed and forbidden instinctual wishes, and it is this punishment wish which appears in the manifest content of the dream.[2, 3]

(c) Bodily needs occuring during the night may give rise to wishes which may be presented as fulfilled in the dream, or in some way woven into the manifest content of the dream. Such wishes are not in themselves sufficient to form a dream.[4]

[1] (1900a) *The Interpretation of Dreams*, S.E., Vol. 5, pp. 551–4.
[2] [1919 addition] ibid., pp. 556–8.
[3] (1933a) *New Introductory Lectures on Psycho-Analysis*. S.E., Vol. 22, p. 27 f.
[4] (1900a) *The Interpretation of Dreams*, S.E., Vol. 5, pp. 551–3.

NOTE ON FREUD'S USE OF THE TERMS 'LATENT DREAM-CONTENT' AND 'LATENT DREAM-THOUGHTS'

Some confusion may arise from Freud's use of the terms 'latent dream content' and 'latent dream-thoughts'. Strictly speaking, the term 'latent dream content' refers to all parts of a dream which are not manifest but are only discovered through the work of interpretation, including dynamically unconscious wishes, preconscious material, and sensory or somatic stimuli. The term 'latent dream-thoughts', on the other hand, is less comprehensive and refers only to the preconscious components of the latent content. In *The Interpretation of Dreams* in particular he sometimes tended to use these terms interchangeably, at times even explicitly equating them: 'We have introduced a new class of psychical material between the manifest content of dreams and the conclusions of our enquiry: namely, their *latent* content, or (as we say) the "dream-thoughts", arrived at by means of our procedure.'[1] On other occasions, however, he clearly emphasized the restricted sense in which he used the term 'latent dream-thoughts': 'In analysis we make the acquaintance of these "day's residues" in the shape of latent dream-thoughts; and, both by reason of their nature and of the whole situation, we must regard them as preconscious ideas, as belonging to the system *preconscious* . . . these day's residues must receive a reinforcement which has its source in unconscious instinctual impulses if they are to figure as constructors of dreams.'[2]

It should be stressed, however, that where Freud uses the terms interchangeably this is a purely terminological inconsistency and does not reflect any confusion on his part with regard to the conception of the various latent elements which are to be discovered by the interpretation of the manifest dream. Such interpretative work leads to current preoccupations (wishes, anxieties, unsolved

[1] (1900a) *The Interpretation of Dreams*, S.E., Vol. 4, p. 277.
[2] (1917d [1915]) 'A Metapsychological Supplement to the Theory of Dreams' S.E., Vol. 14, p. 224.

problems, etc.) of waking life which, although they may be descriptively unconscious, are dynamically preconscious. Freud mostly, though not consistently, uses the term 'latent dream-thoughts' to refer to such preconscious material. The work of interpretation must proceed further and uncover the dynamically unconscious wish (or wishes) which provides the motive power for the dream, and which can only find expression through the preconscious material, distorted and disguised by the dream-work:

'These day's residues are uncovered by tracing back the manifest dream to the latent dream-thoughts; they constitute portions of the latter and are thus among the activities of waking life—whether conscious or [descriptively] unconscious—which have been able to persist into the period of sleep. . . . These day's residues, however, are not the dream itself: they lack the main essential of a dream. Of themselves they are not able to construct a dream. They are, strictly speaking, only the psychical material for the dream-work, just as sensory and somatic stimuli, whether accidental or produced under experimental conditions, constitute the *somatic* material for the dream-work. . . .

'The present state of our knowledge leads us to conclude that the essential factor in the construction of dreams is an unconscious wish [in the dynamic sense]—as a rule an infantile wish, now repressed—which can come to expression in this somatic or psychical material. . . . The dream is in every case a fulfilment of *this* [dynamically] unconscious wish, whatever else it may contain. . . .

'A psycho-analyst can characterize as dreams only the products of the dream-work: in spite of the fact that the latent dream-thoughts are only arrived at from the interpretation of the dream, he cannot reckon them as part of the dream, but only as part of preconscious reflection.'[1]

This suggests that the term 'latent content'—which is the wider one—covers both the dynamically unconscious wish and the preconscious material, as well as any somatic or sensory stimuli which may enter into the content, though as late as 1933 Freud used the term 'latent dream-thoughts' in this wider sense of 'latent dream

[1] (1913a) 'An Evidential Dream', S.E., Vol. 12, p. 273 f.

content': 'Let us go back once more to the latent dream-thoughts. Their most powerful element is the repressed instinctual impulse which has created in them an expression for itself on the basis of the presence of chance stimuli and by the transference on to the day's residues—though an expression that is toned down and disguised.'[1] However, it is usually quite clear from the context in which sense Freud is using the terms.

[1] (1933a) *New Introductory Lectures on Psycho-Analysis*, S.E., Vol. 22. p. 19.

LATENT DREAM-CONTENT

The latent content of dreams consists of:

1. *Dynamically unconscious wishes* (id impulses) prevented by the censorship (the defences of the ego) from reaching consciousness or even the system preconscious during waking life. Several such wishes may be present in the same dream:

'Dreams frequently seem to have more than one meaning. Not only, as our examples have shown, may they include several wish-fulfilments one alongside the other; but a succession of meanings or wish-fulfilments may be superimposed on one another, the bottom one being the fulfilment of a wish dating from earliest childhood. And here again the question arises whether it might not be more correct to assert that this occurs "invariably" rather than "frequently".'[1]

The majority of these impulses are sexual in nature,[2] and most of them stem from the infantile period of life: 'a dream might be described as *a substitute for an infantile scene modified by being transferred on to a recent experience*. The infantile scene is unable to bring about its own revival and has to be content with returning as a dream.'[3]

2. *Latent dream-thoughts*. These include:

(*a*) current preconscious preoccupations and wishes, or indifferent impressions of waking life which have retained some cathexis during sleep (the day's residues).

'The interruption [of sleep] may proceed from an internal excitation or from an external stimulus ... dreams are instigated by residues from the previous day-thought-cathexes which have not submitted to the general withdrawal of cathexes, but have retained

---

[1] (1900a) *The Interpretation of Dreams*, S.E., Vol. 4, p. 219.

[2] ibid., Vol. 5, p. 396.

[3] ibid., p. 546.

in spite of it a certain amount of libidinal or other interest . . .
these day's residues must receive a reinforcement from unconscious
instinctual impulses if they are to figure as constructors of dreams.'[1]

(b) preconscious thoughts which are linked with earlier experiences:

'If we now bear in mind how great a part is played in the [latent]
dream-thoughts by infantile experiences or by fantasies based
upon them, how frequently portions of them re-emerge in the
dream-content and how often the dream-wishes themselves are
derived from them, we cannot dismiss the probability that in
dreams too the transformation of thoughts into visual images may
be in part the result of the attraction which memories couched in
visual form and eager for revival bring to bear upon thoughts cut
off from consciousness and struggling to find expression.'[2]

3. *Sensory excitations.* Under certain conditions, somatic sources
of stimulation during the night, such as for instance thirst or
sexual excitations, 'are brought in to help in the formation of a
dream if they fit in appropriately with the ideational content
derived from the dream's psychical sources, but otherwise not.'[3]
Such somatic stimuli may form part of the latent content of the
dream if they cannot be ignored or denied; they are then used as
components in the situation wished for in the dream. Otherwise
they do not form part of the latent content but merely act as
dream sources (see concept *Dream Sources*).[4]
Of these three constituents of the latent dream content the
dynamically unconscious wishes are of prime importance. There
can be no dream without a dynamically unconscious (repressed)
wish. Current preoccupations and sensory excitations may instigate
a dream, but only if, through association, they can be linked with
and reinforced by a dynamically unconscious wish:

'. . . wishful impulses left over from conscious waking life must be
relegated to a secondary position in respect to the formation of
dreams. I cannot allow that, as contributors to the content if

---

[1] (1917d [1915]) 'A Metapsychological Supplement to the Theory of Dreams',
S.E., Vol. 14, p. 224.
[2] (1900a) *The Interpretation of Dreams*, S.E., Vol. 5, p. 546.
[3] ibid., Vol. 4, p. 237.
[4] ibid., p. 228 and p. 234 f.

dreams, they play any other part than is played, for instance, by the material of sensations which become currently active during sleep.'[1]

All these components of the latent dream content combine in the dream:

'the dream-work is under the necessity of combining into a unity all instigations to dreaming which are active simultaneously. . . . Thus a dream appears to be a reaction to everything that is simultaneously present in the sleeping mind as currently active material. So far as we have hitherto analysed the material of dreams, we have seen it as a collection of psychical residues and memory-traces, to which (on account of the preference shown for recent and infantile material) we have been led to attribute a hitherto indefinable quality of being "currently active" . . . if fresh material in the form of sensations is added during sleep . . . these sensory excitations . . . are united with the other currently active psychical material to furnish what is used for the construction of the dream.'[2]

In the latent content of every dream there is to be found the fulfilment of a wish, a general rule which also includes the latent content of those dreams whose manifest content is unpleasant or anxiety provoking:

'my theory is not based on a consideration of the manifest content of dreams but refers to the thoughts which are shown by the work of interpretation to lie behind dreams. We must make a contrast between the *manifest* and the *latent* content of dreams . . . it still remains possible that distressing dreams and anxiety dreams, when they have been interpreted, may turn out to be fulfilments of wishes.'[3]

The various components of the latent content of the dream are distorted and transformed by the various modes of operation of the dream work, finally appearing in disguised form in the manifest content of the dream:

'But now that analysts at least have become reconciled to replacing the manifest dream by the meaning revealed by its interpretation,

[1] ibid., Vol. 5, p. 554 (cf. also ibid., Vol. 4, p. 236; (1933a) *New Introductory Lectures on Psycho-Analysis*, S.E., Vol. 22, p. 19).
[2] ibid., Vol. 4, p. 228.
[3] ibid., p. 135.

many of them have become guilty of falling into another confusion which they cling to with equal obstinacy. They seek to find the essence of dreams in their latent content and in so doing they overlook the distinction between the latent dream-thoughts and the dream-work. At bottom, dreams are nothing other than a particular *form* of thinking, made possible by the conditions of the state of sleep. It is the *dream-work*, which creates that form, and it alone is the essence of dreaming—the explanation of its peculiar nature.'[1]

Hence repressed wishes, for instance, can only enter consciousness by making use of preconscious material and/or nocturnal sensory excitations to evade the censorship:

'dreams are given their shape in individual human beings by the operation of two psychical forces (or we may describe them as currents or systems); and that one of these forces constructs the wish which is expressed by the dream, while the other exercises a censorship upon this dream-wish and, by the use of that censorship, forcibly brings about a distortion in the expression of the wish.'[2]

Consequently, it is the latent content, not the manifest one, which contains the meaning of the dream. Several latent elements may be expressed in one manifest element of the dream, and vice versa. As Freud puts it: 'Not only are the elements of a dream determined by the dream-thoughts many times over, but the individual dream-thoughts are represented in the dream by several elements.'[3]

Affects in dreams belong to the latent content, not the manifest one.[4] (For the vicissitudes of affects in dreams see the concept on *Affects in Dreams*.)

---

[1] [1925] (1900a) *The Interpretation of Dreams*, S.E., Vol. 5, p. 506 f., n. 2 (cf. also ibid., Vol. 4, p. 144 and Vol. 5, p. 507).
[2] ibid., Vol. 4, p. 144 (cf. also (1917d [1915]) 'A Metapsychological Supplement to the Theory of Dreams', S.E., Vol. 14, p. 224, and (1933a) *New Introductory Lectures on Psycho-Analysis*, S.E., Vol. 22, p. 19).
[3] ibid., p. 284.
[4] ibid., Vol. 5, p. 466 f.

LATENT DREAM-THOUGHTS

Latent dream-thoughts is the term used by Freud to describe preconscious thoughts which the dream makes use of as material for its construction. 'The dream-thoughts are entirely rational and are constructed with an expenditure of all the psychical energy of which we are capable. They have their places among thought-processes that have not become conscious—processes from which, after some modification, our conscious thoughts, too, arise.'[1] Similarly: 'The dream-thoughts which we arrive at by means of analysis reveal themselves as a psychical complex of the most intricate possible structure. Its portions stand in the most manifold logical relations to one another: they represent foreground and background, conditions, digressions and illustrations, chains of evidence and counter-arguments.'[2]

They are only distinguished from the vast store of preconscious thoughts of any individual by their suitability for the formation of a dream. Otherwise they are in no way different from other pre-conscious thoughts. The latent dream-thoughts as such do not form part of the manifest dream but are only part of preconscious reflection.[3] Furthermore, he stated: .

'There is no need to assume, however, that this activity of thought is performed during sleep—a possibility which would gravely confuse what has hitherto been our settled picture of the psychical state of sleep. On the contrary, these thoughts may very well have originated from the previous day, they may have proceeded unobserved by our consciousness from their start, and may already have been completed at the onset of sleep.'[4] And: 'We also describe

[1] (1900a) *The Interpretation of Dreams*, S.E., Vol. 5, p. 506.
[2] (1901a) *On Dreams*, S.E., Vol. 5, p. 660, cf. also (1900a) *The Interpretation of Dreams*, S.E., Vol. 5, p. 592 f., and (1900a) *The Interpretation of Dreams*, S.E., Vol. 4 and 5, pp. 123, 311, 312, 468, 589, 593, and (1905c) *Jokes and their Relation to the Unconscious*, S.E., Vol. 8, pp. 28, 160, and (1913j) 'The Claims of Psycho-Analysis to Scientific Interest', S.E., Vol. 13, p. 170, and (1923a) 'Two Encyclopaedia Articles', S.E., Vol. 18, p. 241.
[3] (1913a) 'An Evidential Dream', S.E., Vol. 12, p. 274.
[4] (1900a) *The Interpretation of Dreams*, S.E., Vol. 5, p. 593.

the latent dream-thoughts, on account of their connection with waking life, as *"residues of the [previous] day"*.[1]

Because of their connection with the preconscious and conscious mental activities of the previous day or days they can be influenced or suggested by the analyst.[2] Freud made it clear that the 'latent dream-thoughts' must be distinguished from the 'manifest content of the dream'. He said: '. . . the latent dream-thoughts are not conscious before an analysis has been carried out, whereas the manifest content of the dream is consciously remembered . . .'[3]

Topographically speaking the latent dream-thoughts belong to the system preconscious: '. . . the process of forming dreams is obliged to attach itself to dream-thoughts belonging to the pre-conscious system'.[4] In short the latent dream-thoughts are descriptively unconscious and in the topographical sense are ascribed to the preconscious.

In contrast to the manifest content the latent dream-thoughts themselves have no pictorial character, they acquire it through the activity of the dream work, along 'the path that leads from thoughts to perceptual images, or, . . . from the region of thought-structures to that of sensory perceptions. On this path . . . the dream-thoughts are given a pictorial character; and eventually a plastic situation is arrived at which is the core of the manifest "dream-picture".'[5]

The 'latent dream-thoughts' are centred in a different way to the manifest content:

'. . . the elements which stand out as the principal components of the manifest content of the dream are far from playing the same part in the dream-thoughts. And, as a corollary, the converse of this assertion can be affirmed: what is clearly the essence of the dream-thoughts need not be represented in the dream at all. The

[1] (1923a) 'Two Encyclopaedia Articles', S.E., Vol. 18, p. 241, cf. also (1907a) *Delusions and Dreams in Jensen's 'Gradiva'*, S.E., Vol. 9, p. 92 f., and (1925d [1924]) *An Autobiographical Study*, S.E., Vol. 20, p. 44.
[2] (1923c) 'Remarks on the Theory and Practice of Dream-Interpretation', S.E., Vol. 19, p. 114.
[3] (1900a) *The Interpretation of Dreams*, S.E., Vol. 4, p. 144, cf. also (1910a [1909]) 'Five Lectures on Psycho-Analysis', S.E., Vol. 11, p. 35, and (1913j) 'The Claims of Psychoanalysis to Scientific Interest', S.E., Vol. 13, p. 170.
[4] (1900a) *The Interpretation of Dreams*, S.E., Vol. 5, p. 541.
[5] (1905c) *Jokes and their Relation to the Unconscious*, S.E., Vol. 8, p. 162.

dream is, as it were, differently centred from the dream-thoughts—its content has different elements as its central point.'[1] And:

'The essential elements in a dream are the dream-thoughts, and these have meaning, connection and order. But their order is quite other than that remembered by us as present in the manifest dream. In the latter the connection between the dream-thoughts has been abandoned and may either remain completely lost or be replaced by the new connection exhibited in the manifest content.'[2]

Moreover, a single latent dream-thought is usually represented by several elements of the manifest content, and the converse holds true as well.

'The nature of the relation between dream-content and dream-thoughts thus becomes visible. Not only are the elements of a dream determined by the dream-thoughts many times over, but the individual dream-thoughts are represented in the dream by several elements. Associative paths lead from one element of the dream to several dream-thoughts, and from one dream-thought to several elements of the dream. Thus a dream is not constructed by each individual dream-thought, or group of dream-thoughts . . . [but] . . . rather, by the whole mass of dream-thoughts being submitted to a sort of manipulative process in which those elements which have the most numerous and strongest supports acquire the right of entry into the dream-content.'[3]

This explains the fact that a dream can have many meanings which may be already inherent in the latent dream-thoughts themselves. '. . . one must become accustomed to a dream being thus capable of having many meanings. Moreover, the blame for this is not always to be laid upon incompleteness of the work of interpretation; it may just as well be inherent in the latent dream-thoughts themselves.'[4]

Whereas the ideational material of the latent dream-thoughts undergoes considerable modifications according to the laws of the *dream-work*, affects present in the dream-thoughts either remain unaltered, or are reduced to nothing or turned into their opposite.[5]

[1] (1900a) *The Interpretation of Dreams*, S.E., Vol. 4, p. 305.

[2] (1912–13) *Totem and Taboo*, S.E., Vol. 13, p. 94 f.

[3] (1900a) *The Interpretation of Dreams*, S.E., Vol. 4, p. 284, cf. also (1901a) *On Dreams*, S.E., Vol. 5, p. 653.

[4] (1925i) 'Some Additional Notes upon Dream-Interpretation as a Whole', S.E., Vol. 19, p. 130.

[5] (1900a) *The Interpretation of Dreams*, S.E., Vol. 5, pp. 460, 471.

Intellectual operations (such as judgements, conclusions, cal-culations, etc.), which appear in the manifest content, are taken over from the latent dream-thoughts.

'Everything that appears in dreams as the ostensible activity of the function of judgement is to be regarded not as an intellectual achievement of the dream-work but as belonging to the material of the dream-thoughts and as having been lifted from them into the manifest content of the dream as a ready-made structure. I can even carry this assertion further. Even the judgements made *after waking* upon a dream that has been remembered, and the feelings called up in us by the reproduction of such a dream, form part, to a great extent, of the latent content of the dream and are to be included in its interpretation.'[1]

The latent dream-thoughts constitute only a class of psychical material between the manifest content and the meaning of a dream. They are of particular significance because the dream's meaning (the expression of a wish-fulfilment) can be inferred from them. 'It is from these dream-thoughts and not from a dream's manifest content that we disentangle its meaning.'[2] The interpretations of the latent dream-thoughts first reveals the preconscious *dream-wish* which resulted from the cathexis of preconscious thoughts or wishes by an unconscious (repressed) wish (or wishes). It is the action of such an unconscious wish upon the consciously rational material of the latent dream-thoughts which initiates dream-formation by turning that material into a wish-fulfilment. (See Concept: The Dream Wish.) Unless the day's residues of the dream-thoughts receive such reinforcement from unconscious instinctual impulses they cannot figure as constructors of dreams. In this way 'a train of thought comes into being in the preconscious which is without a preconscious cathexis but has received a cathexis from an unconscious wish,'[3] thus leading to the formation of the dream-wish, i.e. the one represented in the dream as fulfilled. 'But in order for a dream to develop out of them [the latent dream-thoughts], the co-operation of a wish (usually an unconscious one)

[1] (1900a) *The Interpretation of Dreams*, S.E., Vol. 5, p. 445, cf. also (1901a) *On Dreams*, S.E., Vol. 5, p. 667 f.
[2] (1900a) *The Interpretation of Dreams*, S.E., Vol. 4, p. 277, cf. also (1925d [1924]) *An Autobiographical Study*, S.E., Vol. 20, p. 44.
[3] (1900a) *The Interpretation of Dreams*, S.E., Vol. 5, p. 595.

is required; this contributes the motive force for constructing the dream, while the day's residues provide the material.'[1]

The wish uncovered by means of the latent dream-thoughts, having been in a state of repression, is derived from infancy, either from actual infantile experiences or from wishful fantasies (*dream-fantasies*) based upon them which are present in the dream-thoughts in a preconstructed form. The analysis of a dream only gives the content of the latent dream-thoughts, not however, an immediate indication of whether it is based on real or imaginary events. This still remains to be determined: '. . . an analysis only gives us the *content* of a thought and leaves it to us to determine its reality. Real and imaginary events appear in dreams at first sight as of equal validity.'[2]

[1] (1907a) *Delusions and Dreams in Jensen's 'Gradiva'*, S.E., Vol. 9, p. 92 f., cf. also (1917d [1915]) 'A Metapsychological Supplement to the Theory of Dreams', S.E., Vol. 14, p. 226, and (1900a) *The Interpretation of Dreams*, S.E., Vol. 5, p. 594 f.
[2] (1900a) *The Interpretation of Dreams*, S.E., Vol. 4, p. 288.

DAY'S RESIDUES

The Day's Residues are affectively cathected thought processes from the dream-day which have resisted the general lowering of energy through sleep and which, consequently, play the role of dream instigators. They are uncovered by tracing back the manifest dream to the latent dream-thoughts. They constitute portions of the latter[1] but are distinguished from them by their resistance to de-cathexis during sleep. They 'have the most numerous and varied meanings: they may be wishes or fears that have not been disposed of, or intentions, reflections, warnings, attempts at adaptation to current task'. However, 'of themselves they are unable to construct a dream. They are, strictly speaking, only the psychical material for the dream-work, just as sensory and somatic stimuli . . . constitute the somatic material for dream-work.'[2]

Day's residues are essential ingredients in the formation of dreams.[3] In almost every dream is incorporated a memory trace of, or an allusion to an event of the previous day: '. . . for experience has taught us that almost every dream includes the remains of a memory or an allusion to some event (or often to several events) of the day before the dream, and, if we follow these connections, we often arrive with one blow at the transition from the apparently far remote dream-world to the real life of the patient.'[4]

Day's residues are not the motive force of the dream; this is provided by the unconscious wish. Freud compares the day's residues with an entrepreneur in a dream who might have an idea and initiative to carry it through, but can do nothing without capital, and the unconscious wish—with the capitalist who provides the psychical outlay for the dream.[5]

In explaining why recent, and often most trivial, impressions are woven into dreams Freud refers to the psychology of neuroses

[1] (1913a) 'An Evidential Dream', S.E., Vol. 12, p. 273.
[2] ibid., p. 274.
[3] (1900a) *The Interpretation of Dreams*, S.E., Vol. 5, p. 562.
[4] (1933a) *New Introductory Lectures on Psycho-Analysis*, S.E., Vol. 22, p. 11.
[5] (1900a) *The Interpretation of Dreams*, S.E., Vol. 5, p. 561.

from which we know that an unconscious (repressed) idea as such is incapable of entering the preconscious. It can only exercise any effect there by establishing connections with an idea which already belongs to the preconscious, by transferring its intensity on to it and by getting 'covered' by it. This Freud calls 'transference'[1] a term which later came to denote a somewhat different process and which at present one would probably call 'displacement'. The unconscious prefers to weave its action round ideas which had no attention paid to them or those which have had attention promptly withdrawn from them.

The frequency of recent and indifferent elements in dreams is explained by the fact that they have least to fear from the censorship. This explains especially the preference for *trivial* elements. The regular appearance of *recent* elements in dreams points to a need for transference (displacement).[2] 'Both groups of impressions satisfy the demand of the repressed for material that is still clear of associations—the indifferent ones because they have given no occasion for formation of many ties and recent ones because they have not yet had time to form them'.

The impression of the dream-day which instigated the dream may be an important one, in that case we rightly speak of the dream as carrying on with the significant interests of our waking life. As a rule, however, that impression is so trivial, insignificant and unmemorable, that it is only with difficulty that we can recall it.[3] Nevertheless, analysis invariably reveals that a *significant experience*, and one by which the dreamer had good reasons to be stirred, had been replaced by the indifferent one with which it has numerous associative links. These displacements are either a part of the dream-work as such, or they can take place during waking life, before the production of the dream. 'Dreams are never concerned with things which we should not think it worth while to be concerned with during the day, and trivialities which do not affect us during the day are unable to pursue us in our sleep.'[4]

Writing at a later stage, Freud formulated in structural terms what part the day's residues and instinctual wishes played. He stated that dreams may arise either from the id or from the ego,

[1] ibid., p. 562.
[2] ibid., pp. 563–4.
[3] ibid., pp. 655–6.
[4] ibid., p. 656.

i.e. that they might be provoked either by an instinctual impulse (unconscious wish) or by desire left over from waking life, a preconscious chain of thoughts which obtains reinforcement from an unconscious element.[1] In the same publication Freud remarked that in dreams arising from day's residues which have not been dealt with and which merely receive reinforcement from the unconscious, it is often difficult to detect the unconscious motive force and its wish fulfilment; 'but we may assume that it is always there'—he concluded.[2]

[1] (1940a [1938]) *An Outline of Psycho-Analysis*, S.E., Vol. 23, p. 27.
[2] ibid., p. 11.

AFFECTS IN DREAMS

When discussing the vicissitudes of affects in dreams Freud's evaluations are based on a comparison of the affects present in the manifest content with those attached to the latent dream-thoughts. He considered affects in dreams as one of the most reliable means towards the understanding of the meaning of dreams, since they undergo less modification than the ideational content of dream-thoughts, and are less influenced by the censorship.

'In the case of a psychical complex which has come under the influence of the censorship imposed by resistance, the *affects* are the constituent which is least influenced and which alone can give us a pointer as to how we should fill in the missing thoughts . . . the release of affect and the ideational content do not constitute the indisoluble organic unity as which we are in the habit of treating them, but . . . these two separate entities may be merely *soldered* together . . .'[1]

'The detachment of affects from the ideational material which generated them is the most striking thing which occurs to them during the formation of dreams; but it is neither the only nor the most essential alteration undergone by them on their path from the dream-thoughts to the manifest dream.'[2]

For the sake of clarity, the qualitative and quantitative changes undergone by affects in dreams are here discussed separately. In reality, of course, an affect in a dream may undergo both quantitative and qualitative changes.

Quantitative Changes
From the point of view of quantity the possibilities range from complete suppression—mostly in the case of unpleasurable affects —to an intensity which is greater than the ideational content would lead one to expect. But in general dreams are poorer in affect than the psychical material out of which they have been created.

[1] (1900a) *The Interpretation of Dreams*, S.E., Vol. 5, p. 461 f.
[2] ibid., p. 466 f.

THE THEORY OF DREAMS

'The dream-work may succeed in replacing all the distressing ideas by contrary ones and in suppressing the unpleasurable affects attaching to them. The result will be a straightforward dream of satisfaction, a palpable "wish-fulfilment" . . .'[1]

'If we compare the affects of the dream-thoughts with those in the dream, one thing at once becomes clear. Whenever there is an affect in the dream, it is also to be found in the dream thoughts. But the reverse is not true. A dream is in general poorer in affect than the psychical material from the manipulation of which it has proceeded. . . .

' . . . The dream-work has reduced to a level of indifference not only the content but often the emotional tone of my thoughts as well. It might be said that the dream work brings about a *suppression of affects.* . . .

'Things can be otherwise: lively manifestations of affect can make their way into the dream itself.'[2]

Freud ascribes the quantitative reduction of affect to three possible causes: (*a*) the state of sleep itself; (*b*) the censorship; (*c*) the inhibitory effect of contradictory affects.

'I am compelled . . . to picture the release of affects as a centrifugal process directed towards the interior of the body and analogous to the processes of motor and secretory innervation. Now just as in the state of sleep the sending out of motor impulses towards the external world appears to be suspended, so it may be that the centrifugal calling-up of affects by unconscious thinking may become more difficult during sleep. In that case the affective impulses occurring during the course of the dream-thoughts would from their very nature be weak impulses, and consequently those which found their way into the dream would be no less weak. . . . We must also bear in mind that any relatively complex dream turns out to be a compromise produced by a conflict between psychical forces. For one thing, the thoughts constructing the wish are obliged to struggle against the opposition of a censoring agency; and for another thing, we have often seen that in unconscious thinking itself every train of thought is yoked with its contradictory opposite. Since all of these trains of thought are

[1] [1919] ibid., p. 556.
[2] ibid., p. 467.

capable of carrying an affect, we shall by and large scarcely be wrong if we regard the suppression of affect as a consequence of the inhibition which these contraries exercise upon each other and which the censorship exercises upon the impulsions suppressed by it. *The inhibition of affect, accordingly, must be considered as the second consequence of the censorship of dreams, just as dream-distortion is its first consequence.*[1]

The opposite result—an increase in the intensity of the affect—is brought about when affects in dreams are fed from a confluence of several sources and are overdetermined in their reference to the material of the dream-thoughts. This process allows affects attached to sources objectionable to the censorship to avoid the censorship by joining with affects from unobjectionable sources which can screen them. Unobjectionable trains of thought may also provide a screen for affects whose real source is a forbidden infantile wish, though in such cases the screening need not be accompanied by intensification of affect.[2]

'. . . This satisfaction which had escaped censorship had received an accession from another source. This other source had grounds for fearing the censorship, and its affect would undoubtedly have aroused opposition if it had not covered itself by the similar, legitimate affect of satisfaction, arising from the permissible source, and slipped in, as it were, under its wing.'[3]

'In cases such as this the affect is justified in its *quality* but not in its *amount*; and self-criticism which is set at rest on the one point is only too apt to neglect examination of the second one.'[4]

'A satisfaction which is exhibited in a dream and can, of course, be immediately referred to its proper place in the dream-thoughts is not always completely elucidated by this reference alone. It is as a rule necessary to look for *another* source of it in the dream-thoughts, a source which is under the pressure of the censorship. As a result of that pressure, this source would normally have produced, not satisfaction, but the contrary affect. Owing to the presence of the first source of affect, however, the second source

[1] ibid., p. 467 f.
[2] ibid., pp. 478–84.
[3] ibid., p. 478.
[4] ibid., p. 479.

is enabled to withdraw its affect of satisfaction from repression and allow it to act as an intensification of the satisfaction from the first source. Thus it appears that affect in dreams are fed from a confluence of several sources and are over-determined in their reference to the material of the dream-thoughts. *During the dream work, sources of affect which are capable of producing the same affect come together in generating it.'*[1]

Discussing a dream in which an egoistic train of thought had not been censored, and satisfaction had not been turned into un-pleasure,[2] Freud said,

'The explanation was, I think, that other, unobjectionable, trains of thought in connection with the same people found simultaneous satisfaction and screened with *their* affect the affect which arose from the forbidden infantile source.'[3]

In the case of intense affects of a distressing nature which threaten to overwhelm the censor anxiety may be developed and lead to awakening.[4]

Qualitative Changes

From the point of the quality of affects in regard to the ideational contents to which they are attached in dreams we encounter two possibilities, apart from such examples where the affective quality meets our expectations: (*a*) The dream's ideational content is not accompanied by the affects which we would expect from waking life, and (*b*) affects appear in connection with subject-matter which seems to provide no occasion for any such expression.

'It has always been a matter for surprise that in dreams the ideational content is not accompanied by the affective conse-quences that we should regard as inevitable in waking thought. . . . But there is no lack in dreams of instances of a contrary kind, where an intense expression of affect appears in connection with subject-matter which seems to provide no occasion for any such expression. . . .

'This particular enigma of dream-life vanishes more suddenly, perhaps, and more completely than any other, as soon as we pass

[1] ibid., p. 480.
[2] ibid., pp. 480–5.
[3] ibid., p. 486.
[4] [1919] ibid., p. 556 f.

over from the manifest to the latent content of the dream. We need not bother about the enigma, since it no longer exists. Analysis shows us that *the ideational material has undergone displacements and substitutions, whereas the affects have remained unaltered.*'[1]

Because affects undergo less distortion than the ideational material to which they were attached affect often remains in tune with the wish expressed in the dream, not with its disguise.[2]

'In some dreams the affect does at least remain in contact with the ideational material which has replaced that to which the affect was originally attached. In others, the dissolution of the complex has gone further. The affect makes its appearance completely detached from the idea which belongs to it and is introduced at some other point in the dream, where it fits in with the new arrangement of the dream-elements.'[3]

'Just as ideas of things can make their appearance in dreams turned into their opposite, so too can the *affects* attaching to dream-thoughts; and it seems likely that this reversal of affect is brought about as a rule by the dream-censorship. . . . Nor is it necessary to assume, in such cases either, that the dream work *creates* contrary affects of this kind out of nothing; it finds them as a rule lying ready to hand in the material of the dream-thoughts, and merely intensifies them with the psychical force arising from a motive of defence, till they can predominate for the purposes of dream-formation.'[4]

[1] ibid., p. 460.
[2] ibid., p. 463.
[3] ibid., p. 463.
[4] ibid., p. 471 f.

THE USE OF MEMORIES IN DREAMS

Freud regarded it an undisputed fact that 'all the material making up the content of a dream is in some way derived from experience, that is to say, has been reproduced or remembered in the dream'.[1] As he points out elsewhere, 'dreaming is another kind of remembering, though one that is subject to the conditions that rule at night and to the laws of dream-formation'.[2] Of principal importance for the way in which memories are used in dreams is the fact of the lowering of the censorship during the state of sleep. This allows for a considerable increase in the mutual influence which unconscious and preconscious contents exercise upon each other.

While the availability of memories during waking life is dependent upon and considerably restricted by the operation of the censorship (repression and defences in general) so that a vast store of past memories is no longer available to our waking thoughts under normal conditions, the state of sleep and the special conditions obtaining during it make the whole store of past memories potentially available for use in dreams. This applies particularly to memories which had been subjected to repression. Such memories are, of course, subjected to the distortions of the dream-work (see Concept on *Dream-Work*) and appear in disguised form in the manifest content. But Freud also refers to those dreams whose manifest content contain indications that 'we know and remembered something which was beyond the reach of our waking memory'.[3] Elsewhere he states that 'no one who occupies himself with dreams can, I believe, fail to discover that it is a very common event for a dream to give evidence of knowledge and memories which the waking subject is unaware of possessing'.[4] Dreams which contain such memories are referred to as ' "hypermnesic" dreams'.[5]

[1] (1900a) *The Interpretation of Dreams*, S.E., Vol. 4, p. 11.
[2] (1918b [1914]) 'From the History of an Infantile Neurosis', S.E., Vol. 17, p. 51.
[3] (1900a) *The Interpretation of Dreams*, S.E., Vol. 4, p. 11.
[4] ibid., p. 14 (cf. also ibid., p. 16).
[5] ibid., p. 13.

48

The interpretation of dreams reveals that the selection of memories used in dreams shows three main characteristics which Freud lists as follows:

'(1) Dreams show a clear preference for the impressions of the immediately preceding days . . .

'(2) They make their selection upon different principles from our waking memory, since they do not recall what is essential and important but what is subsidiary and unnoticed.

'(3) They have at their disposal the earliest impressions of our childhood and even bring up details from that period of life which, once again, strike us as trivial and which in our waking state we believe to have been long since forgotten.'[1]

With regard to the first above characteristic Freud points out that 'in every dream it is possible to find a point of contact with the experiences of the previous day'.[2] (See Concept on *Day's Residues*.)

Freud considered the second feature above as the 'most striking and least comprehensible characteristic of memory in dreams'.[3] He points out 'how the remarkable preference shown by the memory in dreams for indifferent, and consequently unnoticed, elements in waking experience is bound to lead people to overlook in general the dependence of dreams upon waking life and at all events to make it difficult in any particular instance to prove that dependence'.[4] Later he deals with the factors which are responsible for this characteristic of memories in dreams, stating that:

'the fact that the content of dreams includes remnants of trivial experiences is to be explained as a manifestation of dream-distortion (by displacement); and it will be recalled that we came to the conclusion that dream-distortion was the product of a censorship operating in the passage-way between two psychical agencies. It is to be expected that the analysis of a dream will regularly reveal its true, psychically significant source in waking life, though the emphasis has been displaced from the recollection of that source on to that of an indifferent one.'[5]

---

[1] ibid., p. 163 f.
[2] ibid., p. 165.
[3] ibid., p. 18.
[4] ibid., p. 19.
[5] ibid., p. 177.

In a later addition Freud pointed out furthermore that 'it by no means rarely happens that innocent and unimportant actions of the previous day are repeated in a dream. . . . What the dreamer himself is stressing in dreams of this kind is not, however, the content of the memory but the fact of its being "real" '.[1]

With regard to the use of memories from earliest childhood in dreams, Freud states that these form one of the foremost 'sources from which dreams derive material for reproduction—material which is in part neither remembered nor used in the activities of waking thought'.[2] In a later passage Freud points out that 'the fact that dreams are hypermnesic and have access to material from childhood has become one of the corner-stones of our teaching. Our theory of dreams regards wishes originating in infancy as the indispensible motive force for the formation of dreams'.[3]

Memories in dreams are thus basically of three types, namely recent memories (day's residues), unrepressed past memories (as evidenced in hypermnesic dreams), and repressed past memories (which find their way into the manifest content of dreams in a distorted form).

The distortion of memories in dreams is due to the censorship which remains active between the systems preconscious and unconscious and necessitates modifications according to the laws of the dream-work. This means that memories are first subjected to a topographical regression and are subsequently distorted by the primary process phenomena of displacement and condensation. Memories are thus treated in exactly the same way as any other unconscious or preconscious mental content which has retained some cathexis during sleep and contributed to the formation of dreams.

The operation of the dream-work still has a further consequence with regard to the reproduction of memories in dreams, namely that they often appear in them in a fragmented form. Freud supports another writer in this who had pointed out that:

'dreams do not reproduce experiences. They take one step forward, but the next step in the chain is omitted, or appears in an altered form, or is replaced by something entirely extraneous.

[1] [1909] ibid., p. 21, n. 2.
[2] ibid., p. 15.
[3] ibid., Vol. 5, p. 589.

Dreams yield no more than *fragments* of reproductions; and this is so general a rule that theoretical conclusions may be based on it. It is true that there are exceptional cases in which a dream repeats an experience with as much completeness as is attainable by our waking memory.'[1]

[1] ibid., Vol. 4, p. 20 f.

DREAM-FANTASIES

'Dream-Fantasies' is the term utilized by Freud when he described a certain type of dream which impresses us by being particularly well-constructed by its clarity and distinctness. He remarks that in some dreams the clarity or indistinctness of the dream has no connection with the make up of the dream itself (dream-work) but is due to the clarity or indistinctness of the latent dream thoughts themselves. For those reasons he thought of introducing a category of dreams which were not subject to the mechanism of condensation and displacement, to be described as fantasies during sleep. Closer examination showed in these dreams the same gaps and flaws in their structure as in any other. This last consideration made him drop, at the time, such a category of dreams, but in 1930 he added a footnote to the above mentioned where he says, that he is now uncertain about the justification of his having dropped such a category of dream-fantasies.[1]

Freud attributes to the *secondary revision* the capacity to create new contributions to dreams, in trying to produce a more logical and coherent façade for the dream, but like the other factors in the *dream work* it prefers to select from psychical material already formed in the *latent dream thoughts*. In some cases, though, it is spared the labour of building up a *façade* for the dream because among the elements of the *latent dream thoughts* a formation of that kind already exists, that is a *fantasy* (a day-dream of waking life) of which the secondary revision will take possession and will seek to introduce into the content of the dream for the purpose of giving the dream a suitable *façade*.[2]

Freud commented on the fact that it was peculiar to the secondary revision to make welcome use of a ready-made fantasy instead of putting one together out of the material of the dream-thoughts and that this may perhaps help in solving one of the puzzles of

[1] (1922a) 'Dreams and Telepathy', S.E. Vol. 17, p. 208 (cf. also (1900a) *The Interpretation of Dreams*, S.E., Vol. 4, p. 331).
[2] (1900a) *The Interpretation of Dreams*, S.E., Vol. 4, p. 190, n. 2 (cf. also Vol. 5, p. 491 f.).

dreams. That is, does the dream work accelerate our thought activity to a degree that we can not assume in waking life? He uses Maury's guillotine dream to explain this phenomenon and assumes that it represents a fantasy stored up ready made for years that was aroused—or rather 'alluded to'—at the moment in which the piece of wood struck Maury's neck, that is, at the moment at which he became aware of the stimulus that woke him up. Such a long story was composed beforehand and not during the extremely short interval at the dreamer's disposal.[1]

It is not necessary either that the fantasy had been gone through during sleep. It would have been sufficient for it to be merely touched on at some point. This point is the port of entry through which the whole fantasy is put in a state of excitation (it may well be the same in the case of unconscious thinking). The fantasy is not gone through during sleep but only in the recollection of the sleeper after his awakening. After waking he remembers in all its details the fantasy which was stirred up as a whole in his dream. One has no means of assuring oneself in such a case that one is really remembering something one has dreamt.[2] (See Secondary Revision and Fantasies and Dreams.)

[1] ibid., Vol. 5, p. 495 f.
[2] ibid., p. 497.

MANIFEST CONTENT

The manifest content of the dream refers to all aspects of what the dreamer consciously remembers after waking up and is retained in his memory in any given form, e.g. in pictures, incongruous situations, in the form of contradictory emotions, etc.

All the material remembered after waking up however disconnected, confused and meaningless which makes up the manifest content of a dream is in some way derived from experience. These may be infantile experiences or *fantasies* based upon them which re-emerge in the manifest dream content in a disguised form. Freud made it quite clear that his 'theory [of dreams] is not based on a consideration of the manifest content of dreams but refers to the thoughts which are shown by the work of interpretation to lie behind dreams'. He continued, 'We must make a contrast between the *manifest* and the *latent* content of dreams'.[1] The above considerations and those pertaining to the *dream-work* (see this concept) are in fact the essential aspects of his theory.

'As compared with the processes we have come to know in it [in the dream-work], interest in the manifest dream must pale into insignificance.'[2]

He says: 'It is from these dream-thoughts and not from a dream's manifest content that we disentangle its meaning.'[3] Thus the analyst is presented with the task 'of investigating the relations between the manifest content of dreams and the latent dream-thoughts, and of tracing out the processes by which the latter have been changed into the former'.[4]

Freud compares the manifest content in a dream to a picture puzzle which even though assembled in its proper relation of each piece to the others may give a nonsensical impression as a whole. This nonsensical puzzle was woven by the *dream work* and has to be unravelled or translated into another mode of expression.

[1] (1900a) *The Interpretation of Dreams*, S.E., Vol. 4, p. 135 and Vol. 5, p. 643.
[2] (1916–17) *Introductory Lectures on Psycho-Analysis*, S.E., Vol. 15–16, p. 181.
[3] ibid., p. 277.   [4] ibid., p. 277.

The manifest content is expressed as it were in a pictographic script, the characters of which have to be transposed individually into the language of the *dream thoughts*, which is intelligible.[1]

These *latent dream thoughts* are not conscious, whereas the manifest content of the dream is consciously remembered. This conscious memory is a substitute for the latent thoughts and impulses which were allowed by the *censor* to pass and enter consciousness in a distorted and unrecognizable form.[2]

Freud has referred to a group of dreams 'in which the manifest and latent content coincide, and there appears to be a consequent saving in dream-work'. This is the case for example with children's dreams to which he refers as 'simple and undisguised *wish-fulfilments*'.[3]

He adds that 'dreams of this infantile type can be found in adults as well, though, . . . they are usually brief in content'. He is referring to the 'dreams of convenience'[responding to thirst with dreams of drinking, etc.].[4]

While discussing that the final aspect of the manifest content is irrelevant, what is important being the dream-distortion that led to it he said that 'there are other occasions when this facade of the dream *has* its meaning and reproduces an important component of the latent dream-thoughts with little or no distortion'. He continues: 'But we cannot know this before we have submitted the dream to interpretation and have been able to form a judgement from it as to the amount of distortion that has taken place.'[5]

In an addition in 1914 to *The Interpretation of Dreams* Freud refers to Silberer who 'has given examples which show convincingly that in many dreams the last pieces of the manifest content, which are immediately followed by waking, represent nothing more nor less than an intention to wake or the process of waking'.[6] He continued saying that, 'This very interesting functional phenomenon of Silberer's has, through no fault of its discoverer, led to many abuses; for it has been regarded as lending support to the old inclination to give abstract and symbolic interpretations to dreams'.[7]

[1] ibid., p. 277 f.
[2] (1900a) *The Interpretation of Dreams*, S.E., Vol. 4, p. 144 and Vol. 5, p. 641.
[3] (1900a) *The Interpretation of Dreams*, S.E., Vol. 5, p. 643 f.
[4] ibid., p. 645.
[5] (1916–17) *Introductory Lectures on Psycho-Analysis*, S.E., Vol. 15, p. 181.
[6] [1914] (1900a) *The Interpretation of Dreams*, S.E., Vol. 5, p. 504.
[7] ibid., p. 505.

DREAM CENSORSHIP

Nature of the Censorship

Dream-Censorship is the function which controls the expression of unconscious wishes that press towards consciousness and thereby threaten to wake the sleeper. It is one aspect of the process of censorship which also operates during waking life.

'The purposes which exercise the censorship are those which are acknowledged by the dreamer's waking judgement, those with which he feels himself at one.

... The purposes *against* which the dream-censorship is directed must be described in the first instance from the point of view of that agency itself. If so, one can only say that they are invariably of a reprehensible nature, repulsive from the ethical, and social point of view matters of which one does not venture to think at all or thinks only with disgust.'[1]

In his theory of conflict between repressed and repressing forces, Freud saw the censorship as that function of the repressing force which brings about repression, so that he attributed the censorship to different agencies, systems or structures as his ideas developed. In the principal models of the mind, the topographical and structural, the censorship is seen as a function respectively of the system preconscious, and the ego-superego. Reviewing his formulations Freud said, in 1914,

'We did not, however, picture this censorship as a special power, but chose the term to designate one side of the repressive trends that govern the ego, namely the side which is turned towards the dream-thoughts. If we enter further into the structure of the ego, we may recognize in the ego ideal and in the dynamic utterances of conscience the *dream-censor* as well.'[2]

'It is plausible to suppose that the '*dream-censorship*', which we

---

[1] (1916–17) *Introductory Lectures on Psycho-Analysis*, S.E., Vol. 15, p. 139 f.
[2] (1914c) 'On Narcisism: An Introduction', S.E., Vol. 14, p. 97.

regard as being responsible in the first instance for the distortion of the dream-thoughts into the manifest dream, is an expression of the same mental forces which during the day-time had held back or *repressed* the unconscious wishful impulse.'[1]

The Censorship in the State of Sleep
The state of sleep makes possible a partial relaxation of the censorship since unconscious wishes can, no longer find expression through action, but only through hallucination, ' . . . *The state of sleep makes the formation of dreams possible because it reduces the power of the endopsychic censorship*'.[2]

'Now while this agency, in which we recognize our normal ego, is concentrated on the wish to sleep, it appears to be compelled by the psycho-physiological conditions of sleep to relax the energy with which it is accustomed to hold down the repressed material during the day. In itself, no doubt, this relaxation does no harm; however much the suppressed impulses of the childish mind may prance around, their access to consciousness is still difficult and their access to movement is barred, as the result of this same state of sleep. The danger of sleep being disturbed by them must, however, be guarded against.'[3]

'The wish to sleep endeavours to draw in all the cathexes sent out by the ego and to establish an absolute narcissism. This can only partly succeed, for what is repressed in the system unconscious does not obey the wish to sleep. A part of the anticathexis has therefore to be maintained, and the censorship between the unconscious and preconscious must remain, even if not at its full strength. So far as the dominance of the ego extends, all the systems are emptied of cathexes. The stronger the unconscious instinctual cathexes are, the more unstable is sleep.'[4]

The Function of Censorship
The dream censorship functions to preserve sleep by controlling the expression of unconscious wishes, and preventing the generation of unpleasant affect. '*The inhibition of affect . . . must be*

[1] (1923a) 'Two Encyclopaedia Articles', S.E., Vol. 18, p. 242.
[2] (1900a) *The Interpretation of Dreams*, S.E., Vol. 5, p. 526.
[3] (1901a) *On Dreams* S.E., Vol. 5, p. 679.
[4] (1917d) 'A Metapsychological Supplement to The Theory of Dreams', S.E., Vol. 14, p. 225.

considered as the second consequence of the censorship of dreams, just as dream-distortion is its first consequence.[1] It should be noted that while it is the censorship that necessitates dream-distortion, the censorship itself does not actually carry out the distortion. This is done by the dream-work. The work of the censorship is merely to prevent unconscious wishes from entering the preconscious, or from linking up with preconscious wishes. Only if the unconscious wishes can be sufficiently disguised by the dream-work will the censorship permit the compromise formation to be experienced as part of the dream.

'The unconscious impulse makes use of this nocturnal relaxation of repression in order to push its way into consciousness with the dream. But the repressive resistance of the ego is not abolished in sleep but merely reduced. Some of it remains in the shape of a *censorship of dreams* and forbids the unconscious impulse to express itself in the forms which it would properly assume. In consequence of the severity of the censorship of dreams, the latent dream-thoughts are obliged to submit to being altered and softened so as to make the forbidden meaning of the dream unrecognizable. This is the explanation of dream-distortion, which accounts for the most striking characteristics of the manifest dream. We are therefore justified in asserting that *a dream is the (disguised) fulfilment of a (repressed) wish.* It will now be seen that dreams are constructed like a neurotic symptom: They are compromises between the demands of a repressed impulse and the resistance of a censorship force in the ego. . . .

'I have given the name of *dream-work* to the process which, with the co-operation of the censorship, converts the latent thoughts into the manifest content of the dream.'[2]

The censorship may act directly on the content of a dream by means of partial repression of some of the content, resulting in gaps in the dream. But more commonly the working of the censorship is evident only in the distortions brought about by the dream-work.

'Wherever there are gaps in the manifest dream the dream-censorship is responsible for them. We should go further, and

---

[1] (1900a) *The Interpretation of Dreams*, S.E., Vol. 5, p. 468.
[2] (1925d) *An Autobiographical Study*, S.E., Vol. 20, p. 44 f.

regard it as a manifestation of the censorship wherever a dream-element is remembered especially faintly, indefinitely and doubtfully among other elements that are more clearly constructed. But it is only rarely that this censorship manifests itself so un-disguisedly. . . .

'The censorship takes effect much more frequently according to the second method, by producing softenings, approximations and allusions instead of the genuine thing. . . . [A third method is dis-placement of accent] . . . As a result of this displacement of accent, this fresh grouping of the elements of the content, the manifest dream has become so unlike the latent dream-thoughts that no-one would suspect the presence of the latter behind the former.'[1]

Rejection of interpretation of the dream made after waking is also the work of the censorship.

'What we met with as resistance in our work of interpretation must now be introduced into the dream-work in the form of the dream-censorship. The resistance to interpretation is only a putting into effect of the dream-censorship. It also proves to us that the force of the censorship is not exhausted in bringing about the distortion of dreams and thereafter extinguished, but that the censorship persists as a permanent institution which has as its aim the maintenance of the distortion. Moreover, just as the strength of the resistance varies in the interpretation of each element in a dream, so too the magnitude of the distortion introduced by the censorship varies for each element in the same dream.'[2]

The amount of distortion occurring in a given dream is dependent on the wish that has to be censored and on the severity of the demands of the censorship.

'Bear in mind, too, that dream-distortion is proportionate to two factors. On the one hand it becomes greater the worse the wish that has to be censored; but on the other hand it also becomes greater the more severe the demands of the censorship at the moment.'[3]

Failures and Apparent Failures of the Function of Dream-Censorship
Freud discussed anxiety dreams where the censorship fails in its

[1] (1916–17) *Introductory Lectures on Psycho-Analysis*, S.E., Vol. 15, p. 139 f.
[2] ibid., p. 141.　　　　　[3] ibid., p. 143.

function of preventing the generation of unpleasant affect and preserving sleep.

'. . . internal stimuli, caused by instinctual demands, are given free play by the sleeper and allowed to find satisfaction in the formation of dreams, so long as the latent dream-thoughts submit to the control of the censorship. But if they threaten to break free and the meaning of the dream becomes too plain, the sleeper cuts short the dream and wakes in a fright. (Dreams of this class are known as anxiety-dreams.)'[1]

'. . . anxiety-dreams only occur if the censorship has been wholly or partly overpowered; and, on the other hand, the overpowering of the censorship is facilitated if anxiety has already been produced as an immediate sensation arising from somatic sources. We can thus plainly see the purpose for which the censorship exercises its office and brings about the distortion of dreams: it does so *in order to prevent the generation of anxiety or other forms of distressing affect.*'[2]

Sometimes anxiety-arousing dreams can be tolerated and sleep can continue through the introduction into the dream by the censorship of the thought 'it is only a dream'.

'In my view the contemptuous critical judgement, "it's only a dream", appears in a dream when the censorship, which is never quite asleep, feels that it has been taken unawares by a dream which has already been allowed through. It is too late to suppress it, and accordingly the censorship uses these words to meet the anxiety or the distressing feeling aroused by it.'[3]

Some manifestly 'immoral' dreams do not result in the arousal of anxiety and the interruption of sleep, either because the manifest 'immoral' content merely masks a quite different latent content, or because the unconscious wish expressed can be felt as remote, or because it links up with a corresponding worry from waking life.

'If, in the first place, one submits these dreams to interpretation, one finds that some of them have given no offence to the censorship because *au fond* they have no bad meaning. They are

[1] (1925d) *An Autobiographical Study*, S.E., Vol. 20, p. 45.
[2] (1900a) *The Interpretation of Dreams*, S.E., Vol. 4, p. 267.
[3] ibid., S.E., Vol. 5, p. 489.

innocent boastings or identifications that put up a mask of pretence; they have not been censored because they do not tell the truth!'[1]

'In these dreams [of the death of a loved relative] we find the highly unusual condition realized of a dream-thought formed by a repressed wish entirely eluding censorship and passing into the dream without modification. There must be special factors at work to make this event possible, and I believe that the occurrence of these dreams is facilitated by two such factors. Firstly, there is no wish that seems more remote from us than this one: "we couldn't even *dream*"—so we believe—of wishing such a thing. For this reason the dream-censorship is not armed to meet such a monstrosity, just as Solon's penal code contained no punishment for parricide. Secondly, in this case the repressed and unsuspected wish is particularly often met half-way by a residue from the previous day in the form of a *worry* about the safety of the person concerned. This worry can only make its way into the dream by availing itself of the corresponding wish; while the wish can disguise itself behind the worry that has become active during the day.'[2]

Punishment Dreams
Freud discussed a particular type of dream, the punishment dream, where the censorship does not merely bring about the distortion of forbidden unconscious wishes, but actually leads to the construction of a dream expressing the wish that the dreamer be punished for his forbidden impulses.

'Punishment-dreams, too, are fulfilments of wishes though not of wishes of the instinctual impulses but of those of the critical, censoring and punishing agency in the mind. If we have a pure punishment-dream before us, an easy mental operation will enable us to restore the wishful dream to which the punishment-dream was the correct rejoinder and which, owing to this repudiation, was replaced as the manifest dream.'[3]

[1] (1925i) 'Some Additional Notes on Dream-Interpretation as a Whole', S.E., Vol. 19, p. 131 f.
[2] (1900a) *The Interpretation of Dreams*, S.E., Vol. 4, p. 266 f.
[3] (1933a) *New Introductory Lectures on Psycho-Analysis*, S.E., Vol. 22, p. 27 f.

DREAM-WORK

The dream-work is the psychical process which transforms the latent dream content into the manifest content. The modes of transformation are the condensation of the material, the displacement of its cathexes, and its modification into pictorial form and dramatized situations. Usually, but not always, the dream-work concludes with the secondary revision, that is by composing the constituents of the dream into an intelligible and connected whole, referred to as the dream façade. It was only from 1923 onwards that Freud did no longer consider the secondary revision as strictly forming part of the dream-work (see Concept on *Secondary Revision*).

The characteristics of the dream-work are entirely different from those of our waking thought:

'The dream-work is not simply more careless, more irrational, more forgetful and more incomplete than waking thought; it is completely different from it qualitatively and for that reason not immediately comparable with it. It does not think, calculate or judge in any way at all; it restricts itself to giving things a new form. It is exhaustively described by an enumeration of the conditions which it has to satisfy in producing its result. That product, the dream, has above all to evade the censorship, and with that end in view the dream-work makes use of a *displacement of psychical intensities* to the point of a transvaluation of all psychical values. The thoughts have to be reproduced exclusively or predominantly in the material of visual or acoustic memory-traces, and this necessity imposes upon the dream-work *considerations of representability* which it meets by carrying out fresh displacements. Greater intensities have probably to be produced than are available in the dream-thoughts at night, and this purpose is served by the extensive *condensation* which is carried out with the constituents of the dream-thoughts. . . . Only a single portion of the dream-work and one which operates to an irregular degree, the working over of the material by partly aroused waking thought [secondary

62

revision], tallies to some extent with the view which other writers have sought to apply to the entire activity of dream-construction.'[1]

The function of the dream-work is (a) to form out of the latent dream-thoughts the 'preconscious dream-wish . . . which *gives expression to the unconscious impulse in the material of the preconscious day's residues*',[2] and (b) to bring this wish to consciousness, the wish being represented as fulfilled in such a way as to command belief in its reality: 'the hallucinatory wishful psychosis—in dreams or elsewhere—achieves two by no means identical results. It not only brings hidden or repressed wishes into consciousness; it also represents them, with the subject's entire belief, as fulfilled.'[3] The functions of the dream-work are carried out in such a way that what becomes conscious is a *compromise* which satisfies the repressed, dynamically unconscious impulses seeking satisfaction (through the representation of the fulfilled wish) and which also satisfies the censorship (through the disguise of the repressed material contained in this wish), and in this way the main function of dreaming as the guardian of sleep is maintained:

'*Repression—relaxation of the censorship—the formation of a compromise*, this is the fundamental pattern not only for the generation of dreams but of many other psychopathological structures; and in the latter cases too we may observe that the formation of compromises is accompanied by processes of condensation and displacement and by the employment of superficial associations, which we have become familiar with in the dream-work.'[4]

The formation of the dream-wish through the agency of the dream-work necessitates the reversal of progressive excitations so that they pursue a retrogressive course through the system unconscious to the perceptual system which then forces itself upon consciousness. This topographical regression also involves a return to the primitive level of hallucinatory wish-fulfilment:

'What actually happens in dream-formation is a very remarkable and quite unforeseen turn of events. The process, begun in the

[1] (1900a) *The Interpretation of Dreams*, S.E., Vol. 5, p. 507 f.
[2] (1917d [1915]) 'A Metapsychological Supplement to the Theory of Dreams', S.E., Vol. 14, p. 226.
[3] ibid., p. 230.
[4] (1901a) *On Dreams*, S.E., Vol. 5, p. 676 (cf. also ibid. pp. 678 and p. 680).

preconscious and reinforced by the unconscious, pursues a backward course, through the unconscious to perception, which is pressing upon consciousness. This *regression* is the third phase of dream-formation. For the sake of clarity, we will repeat the two earlier ones: the reinforcement of the preconscious day's residues by the unconscious, and the setting up of the dream-wish. . . . The reversal of the course of the excitation from the preconscious to perception is at the same time a return to the early stage of hallucinatory wish-fulfilment.'[1]

In this regressive process thoughts are transformed into images, mainly visual ones, i.e. verbal ideas are reduced to ideas of corresponding things because the process is controlled by considerations of suitability for plastic representation:

'A dream-thought is unusable so long as it is expressed in an abstract form; but when once it has been transformed into pictorial language, contrasts and identifications of the kind which the dream-work requires, and which it creates if they are not already present, can be established more easily than before between the new form of expression and the remainder of the material underlying the dream. This is so because in every language concrete terms, in consequence of the history of their development, are richer in associations than conceptual ones.'[2]

When regression is complete there remains in the unconscious system a series of memory traces of things which are cathected, and it is on these that the primary process works (by condensation of them and displacement of their respective cathexes) until it has shaped the manifest dream-content.

The dream-work is completed by the thought content (the dream-thoughts transformed by regression and worked over into a wish) entering consciousness as a sense-perception with the hallucinatory vividness of reality, undergoing as it does so the secondary revision to which every perceptual content is subject, i.e. filling gaps, adding connecting links, etc.:

'The completion of the dream-process consists in the thought-content—regressively transformed and worked over into a wishful

---

[1] (1917d [1915]) 'A Metapsychological Supplement to the Theory of Dreams', S.E., Vol. 14, p. 227 f.
[2] (1900a) *The Interpretation of Dreams*, S.E., Vol. 5, p. 340.

fantasy—becoming conscious as a sense-perception; while this is happening it undergoes secondary revision, to which every perceptual concept is subject. The dream-wish, as we say, is *hallucinated*, and, as a hallucination, meets with belief in the reality of its fulfilment. . . . The formation of the wishful fantasy and its regression to hallucination are the most essential parts of the dream-work.'[1]

If secondary revision is absent or incomplete, the manifest dream will lack a smooth façade and displays gaps and inconsistencies.

The obscuration of the repressed material, which otherwise would not be admissible to consciousness, thus takes place through the dream-work. The regression to perception, though not strictly forming part of the dream-work itself, is an essential precondition for its operation. All that can be attributed to the dream-work itself is condensation, displacement, plastic representation and, to a lesser extent, secondary revision:

'The dream-work exhibits no activities other than the four that have already been mentioned. If we keep to the definition of "dream-work" as the process of transforming the dream-thoughts into the dream-content, it follows that the dream-work is not creative, that it develops no fantasies of its own, that it makes no judgements and draws no conclusions; it has no functions whatever other than condensation and displacement of the material and its modification into pictorial form, to which must be added as a variable factor the final bit of interpretative revision [secondary revision].'[2]

Judgement, criticism, deductive reasoning, mathematical calculations, conversations, etc., are either the expression of subsequent reflection on the dream or, more frequently, they are part-fragments already existing in the latent dream-thoughts.

The dream-work does not always act with the same force on all the elements of the latent dream-thoughts, so that while some of them will be extremely distorted, others will enter the manifest dream content practically unaltered.

[1] (1917d [1915]) 'A Metapsychological Supplement to the Theory of Dreams', S.E., Vol. 14, p. 229 (cf. also (1933a) *New Introductory Lectures on Psycho-Analysis*, S.E., Vol. 22, p. 19 f).
[2] (1901a) *On Dreams*, S.E., Vol. 5, p. 667.

E

THE THEORY OF DREAMS

Freud also dealt with the question as to the timing of the various aspects of the dream-work (displacement, condensation, possibility of representation) in the formation of dreams:

'We must attempt to determine the stages of regression at which the various transformations of the dream-thoughts take place . . . it can at least be stated with certainty that displacement must take place in the thought-material while it is at the stage of the unconscious processes, while condensation must probably be pictured as a process stretching over the whole course of events till the perceptual region is reached. But in general we must be content to assume that all the forces which take part in the formation of dreams operate simultaneously . . . I should like to venture on the assertion that the process of the dream-work preparatory to the dream must be located in the region of the unconscious . . . there would in all be three stages to be distinguished in the formation of a dream: first, the transplantation of the preconscious day's residues into the unconscious, in which the conditions governing the state of sleep must play a part; then, the dream-work proper in the unconscious, and thirdly, the regression of the dream-material, thus revised, to perception, in which form the dream becomes conscious.'[1]

Elsewhere, Freud deals with the same problem, and he makes it quite clear that the assumption of a strict time-sequence within the process of dream-formation does not meet the actual facts and was only adopted for descriptive purposes. He writes:

'But it seems to me unnecessary to suppose that dream-processes really maintain, up to the moment of becoming conscious, the chronological order in which I have described them: that the first thing to appear is the transferred dream-wish, that distortion by the censorship follows, then the regressive change in direction, and so on. I have been obliged to adopt this order in my description; but what happens in reality is no doubt a simultaneous exploring of one path and another, a swinging of the excitation now this way and now that, until at last it accumulates in the direction that is most opportune and one particular grouping becomes the permanent one . . . the dream-work often requires more than a day

[1] (1905c) *Jokes and their Relation to the Unconscious*, S.E., Vol. 8, p. 164 f.

66

and a night in order to achieve its result; and if this is so, we need no longer feel any amazement at the extraordinary ingenuity shown in the construction of the dream. . . . It is like a firework, which takes hours to prepare but goes off in a moment.'[1]

[1] (1900a) *The Interpretation of Dreams*, S.E., Vol. 5, p. 576.

DISTORTION IN DREAMS

Distortion is the term used by Freud to refer to the process of disguise or dissimulation which occurs before unconscious and preconscious material (*the latent dream content*) can gain access to consciousness in the form of a *manifest dream*: 'Dream-distortion is what makes a dream seem strange and unintelligible to us,'[1] and:

'The study of the dream-work teaches us by an excellent example the way in which the unconscious material from the id (originally unconscious and repressed unconscious alike) forces its way into the ego, becomes preconscious and, as a result of the ego's opposition, undergoes the changes which we know as *dream-distortion*.'[2]

Distortion results partly on the one hand from the translation of preconscious thoughts into an archaic method of expression (including symbolization), governed by the laws of the primary process, in the course of *regression*. Distortion is thus the product of the *dream-work*.[3] It is achieved by the processes of condensation displacement of cathexis[4] representation in pictorial form and of the secondary revision which further disguises the latent content while attempting to give the dream a superficially intelligible and coherent façade. [See: Dream Work.] On the other hand it partly results from the restrictive and critical effects of the *censorship* exercised on the unconscious wishful impulse and its derivatives.[5]

Distortion in dreams becomes necessary because it is a function of the censorship '*to prevent the generation of anxiety or other forms of distressing affect*'.[6] If the repressed wish is insufficiently disguised, the dream is accompanied by anxiety, which then interrupts sleep. He said, 'In their case [anxiety dreams] anxiety

---

[1] (1916–17) *Introductory Lectures on Psycho-Analysis*, S.E., Vol. 15, p. 136.
[2] (1940a [1938]) *An Outline of Psycho-Analysis*, S.E., Vol. 23, p. 165.
[3] (1923a) 'Two Encyclopaedia Articles', S.E., Vol. 18, p. 241 f.
[4] (1900a) *The Interpretation of Dreams*, S.E., Vol. 4, p. 489 f.
[5] (1923a) 'Two Encyclopaedia Articles', S.E., Vol. 18, p. 241 f. See also (1901a) *On Dreams*, S.E., Vol. 5, p. 676.
[6] (1900a) *The Interpretation of Dreams*, S.E., Vol. 4, p. 267.

takes the place of dream-distortion.'[1] When anxiety is avoided by successful distortion of the repugnant material, sleep can continue undisturbed.

Freud further explained that 'the magnitude of the distortion introduced by the censorship varies for each element in the same dream',[2] and that 'dream-distortion is proportionate to two factors. On the one hand it becomes greater the worse the wish that has to be censored; but on the other hand it also becomes greater the more severe the demands of the censorship at the moment'.[3] He notes as well that there may be little or no distortion in dreams occasioned by imperative physical needs in adults.[4]

In the dreams of young children distortion may be minimal, the dreams being 'simple and undisguised wish-fulfilments'.[5] Nevertheless, even in these dreams there is some degree of distortion, in that the wish expressed in the *latent dream thought* is represented as fulfilled.[6]

In dreams, affects are dealt with in special ways that further contribute to the distortion observed in them. For example he pointed out the fact 'that in dreams the ideational content is not accompanied by the affective consequences that we should regard as inevitable in waking thought', while there are instances 'where an intense expression of affect appears in connection with subject-matter which seems to provide no occasion for any such expression'. He explained this puzzling situation by saying:
'This particular enigma of dream-life vanishes ... as soon as we pass over from the manifest to the latent content of the dream. ... Analysis shows us that *the ideational material has undergone displacements and substitutions, whereas the affects have remained unaltered.*'[7]

Distortion can occur at all stages in the formation of a dream and even in the attempt to remember the manifest dream after waking: 'The fact that dreams are distorted and mutilated by memory ... is no more than the last and manifest portion of a

[1] (1901a) *On Dreams*, S.E., Vol. 5, p. 674.
[2] (1916–17) *Introductory Lectures on Psycho-Analysis*, S.E., Vol. 15, p. 141.
[3] ibid., p. 143.
[4] (1900a) *The Interpretation of Dreams*, S.E., Vol. 5, p. 645.
[5] ibid., p. 643. See also Vol. 4, pp. 127–31.
[6] (1916–17) *Introductory Lectures on Psycho-Analysis*, S.E., Vol. 15, p. 129.
[7] (1900a) *The Interpretation of Dreams*, S.E., Vol. 5, p. 460 f.

distorting activity which has been in operation from the very start of the dream's formation.'[1]

The forgetting of dreams, as well as difficulties in the interpretation of them, arises from the continuing resistance of the censorship which was responsible for the distortion in the first place.[2]

[1] ibid., p. 590.
[2] ibid., p. 524 f.

CONSIDERATIONS OF REPRESENTABILITY

Plastic Representation

Representability refers to one of the aspects of the dream-work. It serves the function of modifying thoughts and impulses in such a manner that they are capable of being represented (mostly in visual form) as part of the manifest dream, at the same time serving the interests of the censorship and condensation:

'The advantage, and accordingly the purpose, of such a change jumps to the eyes. A thing that is pictorial is, from the point of view of a dream, a thing that is *capable of being represented*: it can be introduced into a situation in which abstract expressions offer the same kind of difficulties to representation in dreams as a political leading article in a newspaper would offer to an illustrator. But not only representability, but the interests of condensation and the censorship as well, can be the gainers from this exchange. A dream-thought is unusable so long as it is expressed in an abstract form; but when once it has been transformed into pictorial language, contrasts and identifications of the kind which the dream-work requires, and which it creates if they are not already present, can be established more easily than before between the new form of expression and the remainder of the material underlying the dream.'[1]

Whilst it is the principal function of condensation and displacement to distort the content of and the links between the latent dream-thoughts, the process which governs representability is primarily concerned with ensuring that the distorted latent dream-thoughts 'are arranged with a view to being represented in visual pictures'.[2] The psychical material which dreams make use of is, for the purposes of representability, reduced to the most succinct and unified expression possible.

---

[1] (1900a) *The Interpretation of Dreams*, S.E., Vol. 5, p. 349 f.
[2] (1923a) 'Two Encyclopaedia Articles', S.E., Vol. 18, p. 241.

Freud regards considerations of representability as the third important factor of the dream-work (the other two being condensation and displacement) responsible for the transformation and distortion of the dream-thoughts into the manifest dream-content. This third aspect of the dream-work is, for the most part, concerned with

'representability in visual images. Of the various subsidiary thoughts attached to the essential dream-thoughts, those will be preferred which admit of visual representation; and the dream-work does not shrink from the effort of recasting unadaptable thoughts into a new verbal form—even into a less usual one—provided that that process facilitates representation and so relieves the psychological pressure caused by constricted thinking. This pouring of the content of a thought into another mould may at the same time serve the purpose of the activity of condensation and may create connections, which might not otherwise have been present, with some other thought.'[1]

Pictorial representation in dreams is intimately connected with the regression to perception which the state of sleep necessitates. Because the path to motility is blocked, the instinctual impulse—which is contained in the latent dream-thoughts—

'is compelled to take the backwards course in the direction of perception and to be content with a hallucinated satisfaction. The latent dream-thoughts are thus transformed into a collection of sensory images and visual scenes. It is as they travel on this course that what seems to us so novel and so strange occurs to them.'[2]

One of the chief factors contributing to the strange and novel impression which many dreams convey is 'the copious employment of symbols, which have become alien to conscious thinking, for representing certain objects and processes', and this is 'in harmony alike with the archaic regression in the mental apparatus and with the demands of the censorship'.[3] This availability of archaic symbols makes possible the representation of several ideas or thoughts by a single image or word. In this context Freud also points out that

[1] (1900a) *The Interpretation of Dreams*, S.E., Vol. 5, p. 344.
[2] (1933a) *New Introductory Lectures on Psycho-Analysis*, S.E., Vol. 22, p. 19 f.
[3] ibid., p. 20.

'there is no necessity to assume that any peculiar symbolizing activity of the mind is operating in the dream-work, but that dreams make use of any symbolizations which are already present in unconscious thinking, because they fit in better with the requirements of dream-construction on account of their representability and also because as a rule they escape censorship.'[1]

Displacement, too, is facilitated by this 'regard for representability' since one idea or image can be substituted by another if it is associatively connected with it. As a consequence of this, cathexes can be displaced or shifted more readily if the dream-thoughts are represented in a plastic form, and hence the manifest dream appears as a condensed version of the distorted dream-thoughts, sensations and wishes which make up the latent dream-content.[2] 'This is so because in every language concrete terms, in consequence of the history of their development, are richer in associations than conceptual ones.'[3]

The transformation of thoughts or ideas into images follows a regressive path. That is to say, word presentations are taken back to the original, infantile representation of things which correspond to them. Referring to the regression of the preconscious day's residues which takes place in dream-formation, Freud states that 'in this process thoughts are transformed into images, mainly of a visual sort; that is to say, word-presentations are taken back to the thing-presentations which correspond to them, as if, in general, the process were dominated by considerations of *representability*'.[4]

Considerations of representability make it necessary that the dream-work has sufficient flexibility to exchange word-presentation until one is found which is suitable for plastic representation: 'It is very noteworthy how little the dream-work keeps to the word-presentations; it is always ready to exchange one word for another till it finds the expression which is most handy for plastic representation.'[5] In addition to this, 'it is true in general that words are frequently treated in dreams as though they were things, and for

---

[1] (1900a) *The Interpretation of Dreams*, S.E., Vol. 5, p. 349.

[2] ibid., p. 654 f.

[3] ibid., p. 340.

[4] (1917d [1915]) 'A Metapsychological Supplement to the Theory of Dreams', S.E., Vol. 14, p. 228.

[5] ibid., p. 228.

that reason they are apt to be combined in just the same way as presentations of things'.[1]

In the process of topographical regression which takes place in the course of the formation of dreams the fabric of the latent dream-thoughts is resolved into its raw material:

'We call it "regression" when in a dream an idea is turned back into the sensory image from which it was originally derived. . . . If we regard the process of dreaming as a regression occurring in our hypothetical mental apparatus, we at once arrive at the explanation of the empirically established fact that all the logical relations belonging to the dream-thoughts disappear during the dream-activity or can only find expression with difficulty. According to our schematic picture, these relations are contained not in the *first Mnem.* systems but in *later* ones; and in case of regression they would necessarily lose any means of expression except in perceptual images. *In regression the fabric of the dream-thoughts is resolved into its raw material.*'[2]

Freud continues by stating 'that the only thoughts that undergo this transformation [into images] are those which are intimately linked with memories that have been repressed or have remained unconscious'.[3] Freud points out further that in dreams the regressions and transformations of thoughts into images is, in part at least, governed by considerations of representability:

'In these pathological cases of regression as well as in dreams the process of transference of energy must differ from what it is in regressions occurring in normal mental life, since in the former cases that process makes possible a complete hallucinatory cathexis of the perceptual systems. What we have described, in our analysis of the dream-work, as "regard for representability" might be brought into connection with the *selective attraction* exercised by the visually recollected scenes touched upon by the dream-thoughts.'[4]

[1] (1900a) *The Interpretation of Dreams*, S.E., Vol. 4, p. 295 f.
[2] ibid., Vol. 5, p. 543.
[3] ibid., p. 544.
[4] ibid., p. 548.

REGRESSION IN DREAMS

The process of regression described by Freud in Chapter 7 of *The Interpretation of Dreams* concerns the reversal of the normal direction of movement of thought processes by which dream thoughts are given hallucinatory representation. This regression has three aspects, the topographical, temporal and the formal. This type of regression is to be distinguished from the libidinal regression that is seen in the revival of infantile wishes that takes place in dreams. In Chapter 7 Freud describes the mental apparatus, using as a model the concept of the reflex arc. Incoming perceptions (which may be internal or external) are received at one end (in Freud's model, by the system perception) and the normal course of the excitatory process is from this end of the apparatus to the motor and, where conscious discharge takes place (via the system unconscious and preconscious to the conscious). Freud states that the system perception can only receive stimuli, it cannot store memory traces of them. This is done in the series of systems (mnemonical) which lie behind perception. In the course of the individual's development, as well as a store of perceptual contents, associative links between perceptions are recorded. These associative links belong to the later systems, and it is they which make possible secondary process thinking. The earlier mnemonical systems contain no such links, but only primitive memory pictures (thing cathexes rather than word cathexes).[1]

The regression taking place in dreams is the effect of the simultaneous resistance of the censorship which prevents the progress of a thought into consciousness by the normal path (via the preconscious) and the backward pull exercised on it by the unconscious memories.[2]

'. . . The only way in which we can describe what happens in hallucinatory dreams is by saying that the excitation moves in a *backward* direction. Instead of being transmitted towards the

[1] (1900a) *The Interpretation of Dreams*, S.E., Vol. 5, pp. 536–43.
[2] ibid., pp. 544, 547, 573.

motor end of the apparatus it moves towards the sensory end and finally reaches the perceptual system. If we describe as "progressive" the direction taken by psychical processes arising from the unconscious during waking life, then we may speak of dreams as having a "regressive" character.

This regression then is undoubtedly one of the psychological characteristics of the process of dreaming: but we must remember that it does not occur only in dreams. . . .

In the waking state, however, this backward movement never extends beyond the mnemic images; it does not succeed in producing a hallucinatory revival of the *perceptual* images. Why is it otherwise in dreams ? When we were considering the work of condensation in dreams we were driven to suppose that the intensities attaching to ideas can be completely transferred by the dream-work from one idea to another. It is probably this alteration in the normal psychical procedure which makes possible the cathexis of the system perception in the reverse direction, starting from thoughts, to the pitch of complete sensory vividness.'[1]

He continued . . . 'If we regard the process of dreaming as a regression occurring in our hypothetical mental apparatus, we at once arrive at the explanation of the empirically established fact that all the logical relations belonging to the dream-thoughts disappear during the dream-activity or can only find expression with difficulty. According to our schematic picture, these relations are contained not in the *first Mnemic* systems but in later ones; and in case of regression they would necessarily lose any means of expression except in perceptual images. *In regression the fabric of the dream-thoughts is resolved into its raw material.'*[2]

In summary:

'. . . in all probability this regression, wherever it may occur, is an effect of a resistance opposing the progress of a thought into consciousness along the normal path, and of a simultaneous attraction exercised upon the thought by the presence of memories possessing great sensory force . . . in . . . dreams . . . perhaps further facilitated by the cessation of the progressive current which streams in during the daytime from the sense organs: . . . It

[1] ibid., p. 543.
[2] ibid., p. 543.

76

is further to be remarked that regression plays a no less important part in the theory of the formation of neurotic symptoms than it does in that of dreams. Three kinds of regression are thus to be distinguished: (*a*) *topographical* regression, in the sense of the schematic picture of the u-systems which we have explained above; (*b*) *temporal* regression, in so far as what is in question is a harking back to older psychical structures; and (*c*) *formal* regression, where primitive methods of expression and representation take the place of the usual ones. All these three kinds of regression are, however, one at bottom and occur together as a rule; for what is older in time is more primitive in form and in psychical topography lies nearer to the perceptual end.'[1]

He added in the 1919 edition of *The Interpretation of Dreams*:

'Nor can we leave the subject of regression in dreams without setting down in words a notion by which we have already repeatedly been struck and which will recur with fresh intensity when we have entered more deeply into the study of the psycho-neuroses: namely that dreaming is on the whole an example of regression to the dreamer's earliest condition, a revival of his childhood, of the instinctual impulses which dominated it and of the methods of expression which were then available to him.'[2]

In describing the way this happens Freud wrote that the wish seeks to reach consciousness, is blocked by the censorship and thus becomes distorted and further halted 'by the sleeping state of the preconscious. . . . The dream-process consequently enters on a regressive path, which lies open to it precisely owing to the peculiar nature of the state of sleep, and it is led along that path by the attraction exercised on it by groups of memories; some of these memories themselves exist only in the form of visual cathexes and not as translations into the terminology of the later systems. In the course of its regressive path the dream-process acquires the attribute of representability. It has now completed the second portion of its zigzag journey. The first portion was a progressive one, leading from the unconscious scenes or fantasies to the preconscious; the second portion led from the frontier of the censorship back again to perceptions.'[3]

[1] [1914] (1900a) ibid., p. 548.
[2] [1919] (1900a) ibid., p. 548.
[3] (1900a) ibid., p. 574.

Freud compares this regression in dreams with various normal and pathological regressive processes. Intentional recollection and other processes or normal thinking involve a retrogressive movement back to the raw material of memory traces underlying the more complex ideational act. But, in this case, the backward movement does not go beyond the mnemic images, because, in normal thought, *reality testing is not abolished as in dreams*.[1] The formation of a wishful fantasy and its regression to hallucination are also found in certain psychotic states, in which reality testing ceases to function.[1]

The aspects of regression so far mentioned can be seen as a temporary ego regression in that there is regression in modes of expression of thoughts, reality testing ceases to function and gratification is sought in a primitive way, through hallucination. It is to these aspects of regression that Freud devotes much detailed discussion. The libidinal aspects of regression in dreams are covered under the discussion of *dream wishes*. The wishes expressed are mainly infantile ones, belonging to an earlier phase of libidinal development, and dreams return to infantile wishes and situations, which are expressed in infantile ways. The dream is regressive in substance as well as in form, and the mental stimuli which disturb sleep cannot be dealt with without such regression of mental activity.[2]

[1] ibid., pp. 229–34.
[2] (1916–17) *Introductory Lectures on Psycho-Analysis*, S.E., Vol. 15, pp. 177–9.

CONDENSATION IN DREAMS

Condensation is one of the most important mechanisms character-istic of the dream-work[1] and, together with displacement, is a distinguishing mark of primary psychical processes which operate in the system unconscious: 'By the process of *displacement* one idea may surrender to another its whole quota of cathexis; by the process of *condensation* it may appropriate the whole cathexis of several other ideas.'[2] This quotation suggests that displacement and condensation describe two aspects of similar processes, namely that if energy (cathexis) is displaced from an idea (content), this idea loses its power to attract attention to itself. Condensation describes the opposite process, that is how several cathectic intensities (which originally belonged to separate ideas) are drawn together—as a consequence of displacement—behind one single mental content (idea, image) and thus increase its intensity and effectiveness. One of the clearest formulations as to what Freud meant by the concept of condensation, as it applies to dreams, can be found in his *Introductory Lectures* where he states:

'The first achievement of the dream-work is *condensation*. By that we understand the fact that the manifest dream has a smaller content than the latent one, and is thus an abbreviated translation of it. Condensation can on occasion be absent; as a rule it is present, and very often it is enormous. It is never changed into the reverse; that is to say, we never find that the manifest dream is greater in extent or content than the latent one. Condensation is brought about (1) by the total omission of certain latent elements, (2) by only a fragment of some complexes in the latent dream passing over into the manifest one and (3) by latent elements which have something in common being combined and fused into a single unity in the manifest dream.'[3]

[1] (1901a) *On Dreams*, S.E., Vol. 5, p. 653.
[2] (1915e) 'The Unconscious', S.E., Vol. 14, p. 186 (cf. also ibid., p. 199).
[3] (1916–17) *Introductory Lectures on Psycho-Analysis*, S.E., Vol. 15, p. 171 (cf. also (1900a) *The Interpretation of Dreams*, S.E., Vol. 4, p. 279).

The function of condensation as part of the dream-work is to intensify certain ideas amongst the latent dream-thoughts, a process which is repeated several times and through which 'the intensity of a whole train of thought may eventually be concentrated in a single ideational element. Here we have the fact of "compression" or "condensation", which has become familiar in the dream-work'.[1]

'The direction in which condensations in dreams proceed is determined on the one hand by the rational preconscious relations of the dream-thoughts, and on the other by the attraction exercised by visual memories in the unconscious. The outcome of the activity of condensation is the achievement of the intensities required for forcing a way through into the perceptual systems.'[2]

The link with visual memories and the creation of perceptual intensities are characteristics which distinguish processes of condensation and of the dream-work as a whole from waking thought-processes:

'In normal mental life, too, we find ideas which, being the nodal points or end-results of whole chains of thought, possess a high degree of psychical significance; but their significance is not expressed by any feature that is obvious in a *sensory* manner to internal perception; their perceptual presentation is not in any respect more intense on account of their psychical significance.'[3]

Condensation operates along the 'backwards course in the direction of perception' which the state of sleep compels every instinctual impulse and latent dream-thought to take.

'The latent dream-thoughts are thus transformed into a collection of sensory images and visual scenes. It is as they travel on this course that what seems to us so novel and so strange occurs to them. . . . Such of those elements [of the latent dream-thoughts] as allow any point of contact to be found between them are *condensed* into new unities. In the process of transforming the thoughts into pictures, preference is unmistakably given to such as permit of this putting-together, this condensation; it is as though

[1] (1900a) *The Interpretation of Dreams*, S.E., Vol. 5, p. 595.
[2] ibid., p. 596.
[3] ibid., p. 595.

a force were at work which was subjecting the material to compression and concentration.'[1]

Another passage makes it quite explicit that condensation comes to bear on mental content before it has reached the perceptual systems:

'When regression has been completed, a number of cathexes are left over in the system *unconscious*—cathexes of memories of *things*. The primary psychical process is brought to bear on these memories, till, by condensation of them and displacement between their respective cathexes, it has shaped the manifest dream-content.'[2]

It is only as a result of such condensation of content and the acquisition of additional cathectic energies from other contents by means of displacement, that 'the intensities required for forcing a way through into the perceptual systems' are achieved.[3]

'As a result of condensation, one element in the manifest dream may correspond to numerous elements in the latent dream-thoughts; but, conversely too, one element in the dream-thoughts may be represented by several images in the dream.'[4]

With regard to condensation and displacement, the analysis of dreams shows that 'the ideas which transfer their intensities to each other stand in the loosest mutual relations. They are linked by associations of a kind that is scorned by our normal thinking and relegated to the use of jokes'.[5] Furthermore, 'thoughts which are mutually contradictory make no attempt to do away with each other, but persist side by side. They often combine to form condensations, just as though there were no contradiction between them'.[6] The only logical relations favoured by condensation are those of similarity, consonance, and the possession of common attributes. 'The dream-work makes use of such cases as a founda-

---

[1] (1933a) *New Introductory Lectures on Psycho-Analysis*, S.E., Vol. 22, p. 20.
[2] (1917d [1915]) 'A Metapsychological Supplement to the Theory of Dreams', S.E., Vol. 14, p. 228.
[3] (1900a) *The Interpretation of Dreams*, S.E., Vol. 5, p. 596.
[4] (1933a) *New Introductory Lectures on Psycho-Analysis*, S.E., Vol. 22, p. 20 (cf. also (1901a) *On Dreams*, S.E., Vol. 5, p. 652 f.).
[5] (1900a) *The Interpretation of Dreams*, S.E., Vol. 5, p. 596.
[6] ibid., p. 596.

tion for dream-condensation, by bringing together everything that shows an agreement of this kind into a new unity.'[1] This applies particularly to such words 'which originally had a pictorial and concrete significance' but are now used 'in a colourless and abstract sense'.[2] Another characteristic of condensation is to form compromise ideas out of similar elements:

'A similarity of any sort between two elements of the unconscious material—a similarity between the things themselves or between their verbal presentations—is taken as an opportunity for creating a third, which is a composite or compromise idea. In the [manifest] dream-content this third element represents both its components; and it is as a consequence of its originating in this way that it so frequently has various contradictory characteristics.'[3]

Condensation is also responsible for the creation of composite figures in the manifest content, i.e. of new unities containing 'features which are peculiar to one or other of the persons concerned but not common to them'. This applies to names, visual features, gestures, etc. Usually the dream avoids the representation of the common elements which have made the composite figure possible, in order to avoid the censorship, so that the composite figure is constructed by indifferent features of the persons represented in it.[4] This creation of composite figures is well described in the following passage:

'A composite figure ... may look like A perhaps, but may be dressed like B, may do something that we remember C doing, and at the same time we may know he is D. This composite structure is of course, emphasizing something that the four people have in common. ... The process is like constructing a new and transitory concept which has this common element as its nucleus. The outcome of this superimposing of the separate elements that have been condensed together is as a rule a blurred and vague image, like what happens if you take several photographs on the same plate.'[5]

[1] (1901a) On Dreams, S.E., Vol. 5, p. 661 f.
[2] (1900a) The Interpretation of Dreams, S.E., Vol. 5, p. 407.
[3] (1901b) The Psychopathology of Everyday Life, S.E., Vol. 6, p. 58 f.
[4] (1900a) The Interpretation of Dreams, S.E., Vol. 4, pp. 320–2.
[5] (1916–17) Introductory Lectures on Psycho-Analysis, S.E., Vol. 15, p. 171 f.

DISPLACEMENT IN DREAMS

Displacement in dreams refers to one of the mechanisms which form part of the dream-work. 'Dream-displacement and dream-condensation are the two governing factors to whose activity we may in essence ascribe the form assumed by dreams.'[1] As such it is operative in the process of regression to perception which takes place in dreams. Although the concept of displacement was later also used to describe one of the ego's major defence mechanisms, displacement—as far as dreams are concerned—only refers to an aspect of the primary process, characteristic of the system unconscious, which comes to bear on the material of a dream. Here, displacement usually operates together with condensation.

Displacement as an aspect of the primary process is concerned with the vicissitudes of cathectic energies: 'The cathectic intensities [in the unconscious] are much more mobile. By the process of *displacement* one idea may surrender to another its whole quota of cathexis; by the process of *condensation* it may appropriate the whole cathexis of several other ideas.'[2]

Freud refers to displacement in dreams as 'the second achievement of the dream-work',[3] the first being condensation. He goes on to say that displacement—we may add, the dream-work as a whole—is made necessary by the operation of the 'dream-censorship'. Displacement in dreams manifests itself in two ways:

'In the first, a latent element is replaced not by a component part of itself but by something more remote—that is, by an allusion; and in the second, the psychical accent is shifted from an important element on to another which is unimportant, so that the dream appears differently centred and strange.'[4]

Expanding on these two characteristics of displacement in dreams, Freud points out that the allusions employed for dis-

[1] (1900a) *The Interpretation of Dreams*, S.E., Vol. 4, p. 308.
[2] (1915e) 'The Unconscious', S.E., Vol. 14, p. 186.
[3] (1916–17) *Introductory Lectures on Psycho-Analysis*, S.E., Vol. 15, p. 173.
[4] ibid., p. 174.

THE THEORY OF DREAMS

placement in dreams 'are connected with the element they replace
by the most external and remote relations and are therefore
unintelligible', because the 'dream-censorship only gains its end
if it succeeds in making it impossible to find the path back from
the allusion to the genuine thing'.[1] This form of displacement also
facilitates condensation in so far as the allusion may have reference
to several elements of the latent dream-thoughts. Freud refers to
this possibility when he states that displacements 'facilitate
condensation in so far as . . . instead of *two* elements, a single
common element intermediate between them found its way into
the dream'.[2] The displacement of accent in dreams is a unique
feature characteristic of them and 'unheard-of as a method of
expressing thoughts', except occasionally in order to produce a
comic effect.[3]

Processes of dream-displacement in general are governed by
considerations of representability. As Freud puts it: 'the direction
taken by the displacement usually results in a colourless and
abstract expression in the dream-thought being exchanged for a
pictorial and concrete one' so that it becomes 'a thing that is
capable of being represented'.[4] The fact 'that the intensities attaching
to ideas can be completely transferred [displaced] by the dream-
work from one idea to another . . . probably . . . makes possible
the cathexis of the system perception in the reverse direction,
starting from thoughts, to the pitch of complete sensory vividness'.[5]

Displacement as part of the dream-work makes possible

'The selection of ideas which are sufficiently remote from the
objectionable one for the censorship to allow them to pass, but
which are nevertheless derivatives of that idea and have taken over
its psychical cathexis by means of a complete transference. For
this reason displacements are never absent in a dream . . .'[6]

In *The Interpretation of Dreams* Freud points out that displacement refers to a shifting of 'psychical value', 'psychical intensities',
or 'degree of interest' attached to particular dream-thoughts. In

[1] ibid., p. 174.
[2] (1900a) *The Interpretation of Dreams*, S.E., Vol. 5, p. 339.
[3] (1916–17) *Introductory Lectures on Psycho-Analysis*, S.E., Vol. 15, p. 174.
[4] (1900a) *The Interpretation of Dreams*, S.E., Vol. 5, p. 339 f.
[5] ibid., p. 543 (cf. also ibid., S.E., Vol. 4, p. 177).
[6] (1905c) *Jokes and their Relation to the Unconscious*, S.E., Vol. 8, p. 171.

84

normal life, predominant ideas have 'acquired a special degree of vividness in consciousness', they have attached to them 'a specially high amount of psychical value—some particular degree of interest'. However,

'in the case of the different elements of the dream-thoughts, a value of this kind does not persist or is disregarded in the process of dream-formation. . . . In the course of the formation of a dream these essential elements, charged, as they are, with intense interest, may be treated as though they were of small value, and their place may be taken in the dream by other elements, of whose small value in the dream-thoughts there can be no question. . . .

'It thus seems plausible to suppose that in the dream-work a psychical force is operating which on the one hand strips the elements which have a high psychical value of their intensity, and on the other hand, *by means of overdetermination,* creates of elements of low psychical value new values, which afterwards find their way into the dream-content. If that is so, *a transference and displacement of psychical intensities* occurs in the process of dream-formation, and it is as a result of these that the difference between the text of the dream-content and that of the dream-thoughts comes about.'[1]

A passage from the *New Introductory Lectures* makes it clearer that the psychical intensities which get displaced during dream-formation are affects separated from the ideational contents of the latent dream-thoughts to which they were originally attached:

'The different ideas in the dream-thoughts are, indeed, not all of equal value; they are cathected with quotas of affect of varying magnitude and are correspondingly judged to be important and deserving of interest to a greater or less degree. In the dream-work these ideas are separated from the affects attaching to them. The affects are dealt with independently. . . . Thus something that played only a minor part in the dream-thoughts seems to be pushed into the foreground in the dream as the main thing, while, on the contrary, what was the essence of the dream-thoughts finds only passing and indistinct representation in the dream. No other part of the dream-work is so much responsible for making the dream

[1] (1900a) *The Interpretation of Dreams*, S.E., Vol. 4, pp. 306–8.

strange and incomprehensible to the dreamer. Displacement is the principal means used in the *dream-distortion* to which the dream-thoughts must submit under the influence of the censorship.'[1]

As Freud pointed out elsewhere,

'the consequence of the displacement is that the dream-content no longer resembles the core of the dream-thoughts and that the dream gives no more than a distortion of the dream-wish which exists in the unconscious.'[2]

Frequently, displacements (and condensations) become operative in the formation of dreams after a topographical regression has taken place through which

'thoughts are transformed into images, mainly of a visual sort; that is to say, word presentations are taken back to the thing-presentations which correspond to them. . . . When regression has been completed, a number of cathexes are left over in the system unconscious—cathexes of memories of *things*. The primary psychical process is brought to bear on these memories, till, by condensation of them and displacement between their respective cathexes, it has shaped the manifest dream-content.'[3]

In considering the effects on a dream of the operation of displacement and condensation, either when they function separately or in combination with each other, Freud points out that when they function separately this leads to the creation of a 'composite idea' in the dream-content which contains common aspects of originally separate dream-thoughts. He gives many examples of this phenomenon,[4] one of which is the following:

'In a dream recorded by Ferenczi . . . , a composite image occurred which was made up from the figure of a *doctor* and of a *horse* and was also dressed in a *night-shirt*. The element common to these three components was arrived at in the analysis after the woman-patient had recognized that the night-shirt was an allusion to her

---

[1] (1933a) *New Introductory Lectures on Psycho-Analysis*, S.E., Vol. 22, p. 20 f.
[2] (1900a) *The Interpretation of Dreams*, S.E., Vol. 4, p. 308.
[3] (1917d [1915]) 'A Metapsychological Supplement to the Theory of Dreams', S.E., Vol. 14, p. 228.
[4] (1900a) *The Interpretation of Dreams*, S.E., Vol. 4, pp. 320–26.

father in a scene from her childhood. In all three cases it was a question of an object of her sexual curiosity.'[1]

However, when 'condensation and displacement *combine* to produce the result', what is produced is not a composite idea but rather something which Freud calls an 'intermediate common entity'. He states:

'if displacement takes place in addition to condensation, what is constructed is not a composite idea but an "intermediate common entity", which stands in a relation to the two different elements similar to that in which the resultant of a parallelogram of forces stands to its components. For instance, in the content of one of my dreams there was a question of an injection with *propyl*. To begin with, the analysis only led me to an indifferent experience which had acted as dream-instigator, and in which a part was played by *amyl*. I was not yet able to justify the confusion between amyl and propyl. In the group of ideas behind this same dream, however, there was also a recollection of my first visit to Munich, where I had been struck by the *Propylaea*. The details of the analysis made it plausible to suppose that it was the influence of this second group of ideas upon the first one that was responsible for the displacement from amyl to propyl. *Propyl* is as it were an intermediate idea between *amyl* and *Propylaea*, and found its way into the content of the dream as a kind of *compromise*, by means of simultaneous condensation and displacement.'[2]

[1] [1911] ibid., p. 325 f.
[2] (1901a) *On Dreams*, S.E., Vol. 5, p. 657.

SECONDARY REVISION

Secondary revision refers to that mental mechanism which fulfils the task of apperceptively structuring and editing both internal and external perceptual phenomena. This secondary revision is an automatic process serving the establishment of logical relationships, links and comprehensibility between disconnected or only loosely linked memories, ideas, perceptions, etc. It is, therefore, of special relevance with regard to dreams, where secondary revision is concerned with the reconstituting of the elements of the dream so that the manifest content will have some semblance, or façade, of logic and coherence:

'In general one must avoid seeking to explain one part of the manifest dream by another, as though the dream had been coherently conceived and was a logically arranged narrative. On the contrary, it is as a rule like a piece of breccia, composed of various fragments of rock held together by a binding medium, so that the designs that appear on it do not belong to the original rocks embedded in it. And there is in fact one part of the dream-work, known as "secondary revision", whose business it is to make something whole and more or less coherent out of the first products of the dream-work. In the course of this, the material is arranged in what is often a completely misleading sense and, where it seems necessary, interpolations are made in it.'[1]

Although secondary revision is of particular importance with regard to dreams and is discussed by Freud predominantly in the context of dream-formation, he is quite explicit about the fact that all perceptual phenomena are subject to secondary revision. He states, for instance, that the 'completion of the dream-process consists in the thought-content . . . becoming conscious as a sense-perception; while this is happening it undergoes secondary revision, to which every perceptual concept is subject.'[2] Another

[1] (1916–17) *Introductory Lectures on Psycho-Analysis*, S.E., Vol. 15, p. 181 f.
[2] (1917d [1915]) 'A Metapsychological Supplement to the Theory of Dreams', S.E., Vol. 14, p. 229.

passage not only re-emphasizes the correspondence between secondary revision in dreams and in waking life, but it also gives a clear exposition of one of the functions fulfilled by this mechanism:

'*Considerations of intelligibility* are what lead to this final revision of a dream; and this reveals the origin of the activity. It behaves towards the dream-content lying before it just as our normal psychical activity behaves in general towards any perceptual content that may be presented to it. It understands that content on the basis of certain anticipatory ideas, and arranges it, even at the moment of perceiving it, on the presupposition of its being intelligible; in so doing it runs a risk of falsifying it, and in fact, if it cannot bring it into line with anything familiar, is a prey to the strangest misunderstandings. As is well known, we are incapable of seeing a series of unfamiliar signs or of hearing a succession of unknown words, without at once falsifying the perception from considerations of intelligibility, on the basis of something already known to us.

Dreams which have undergone a revision of this kind at the hands of a psychical activity completely analogous to waking thought may be described as "well-constructed".'[1]

Freud also made it quite clear that although on the one hand secondary revision serves considerations of intelligibility on a conscious level, it is, as far as dreams are concerned, at the same time in the service of the distortion of the true, unconscious meaning and significance of a dream. Freud refers to this latter function of secondary revision when he states that 'its purpose is evidently to get rid of the disconnectedness and unintelligibility produced by the dream-work and replace it by a new "meaning" '. But this new meaning, arrived at by secondary revision, is no longer the meaning of the dream-thoughts.'[2]

In another passage Freud states that secondary revision constitutes a 'contribution on the part of waking thought to the construction of dreams'.[3]

The fact that secondary revision is intimately linked with waking thought has important implications for the understanding

[1] (1901a) *On Dreams*, S.E., Vol. 5, p. 666 f.
[2] (1912–13) *Totem and Taboo*, S.E., Vol. 13, p. 95.
[3] (1900a) *The Interpretation of Dreams*, S.E., Vol. 5, p. 505 (cf. also ibid., Vol. 4, p. 234).

and interpretation of dreams. Freud draws attention to this when he states that

'There is no doubt . . . that it is our normal thinking that is the psychical agency which approaches the content of dreams with a demand that it must be intelligible, which subjects it to a first interpretation and which consequently produces a complete misunderstanding of it. For the purposes of *our* interpretation it remains an essential rule invariably to leave out of account the ostensible continuity of a dream as being of suspect origin, and to follow the same path back to the material of the dream-thoughts, no matter whether the dream itself is clear or confused.'[1]

Freud makes the same point again when he writes in his paper *On Dreams* where he states that 'the easiest way of forming an idea' of the nature of secondary revision is to suppose 'that *it only comes into operation AFTER the dream-content has already been constructed.* Its function would then consist in arranging the constituents of the dream in such a way that they form an approximately connected whole, a dream-composition.'[2] But Freud goes on to point out that this 'first, preliminary interpretation' or 'dream-façade' does not only consist of 'somewhat arbitrary revisions of the dream-content by the conscious agency of our mental life', but that in 'the erection of a dream-façade use is not infrequently made of wishful fantasies which are present in the dream-thoughts in a pre-constructed form, and are of the same character as the appropriately named "day-dreams" familiar to us in waking life'.[3] (See concept on *Dream-Fantasies*.)

Passages like these suggest what Freud states explicitly when he notes that only after 'a part of the quiescent force of the preconscious' has been set in action by the '*arousing* effect' which every dream has, only after this, is the dream 'submitted by this force to the influence which we have described as secondary revision with an eye to consecutiveness and intelligibility'.[4] But Freud's own uncertainty as to when, in the dream-process, secondary revision becomes operative, is already apparent a few paragraphs later when he suggests that in his opinion 'even the

[1] ibid., p. 500.
[2] (1901a) *On Dreams*, S.E., Vol. 5, p. 666.
[3] ibid., p. 667.
[4] (1900a) *The Interpretation of Dreams*, S.E., Vol. 5, p. 575.

demand for the dream to be made intelligible as a perceptual event [which is the function of secondary revision] may be put into effect before the dream attracts consciousness to itself'.[1] Many years later Freud makes the same point again, this time more emphatically and categorically, when he states that the dream is submitted to the process of secondary revision 'before the manifest dream is arrived at'.[2]

Originally, Freud regarded the process of secondary revision as an integral part of the dream-work. After condensation, displacement, and representability, he considered secondary revision as 'the fourth of the factors concerned in the construction of dreams'.[3] By 1913 he had developed some doubts as to whether secondary revision should strictly be regarded as forming part of the dream-work. He states parenthetically in his article on 'An Evidential Dream':

'Secondary revision by the conscious agency is here reckoned as part of the dream-work. Even if one were to separate it, this would not involve any alteration in our conception. We should then have to say: dreams in the analytic sense comprise the dream-work proper together with the secondary revision of its products.'[4]

Ten years later Freud is quite specific when he states, with reference to secondary revision that 'strictly speaking, this last process does not form part of the dream-work'.[5] Freud did not elaborate on the reasons which prompted him to change his original point of view with regard to secondary revision. But comparing his statements concerning the processes which occur as part of the dream-work on the one hand, and those which characterize secondary revision on the other, one can infer that one of the chief reasons—if not the principal one—for separating secondary revision from the dream-work proper is that the latter functions according to primary process laws, whilst secondary revision is closer to secondary process functioning. Another, but less significant, factor which may have contributed to Freud's separating

---

[1] ibid., p. 576.
[2] (1923a) 'Two Encyclopaedia Articles', S.E., Vol. 18, p. 241.
[3] (1900a) *The Interpretation of Dreams*, S.E., Vol. 5, p. 488. (cf. also ibid., p. 490).
[4] (1913a) 'An Evidential Dream', S.E., Vol. 12, p. 274 f.
[5] (1923a) 'Two Encyclopaedia Articles', S.E., Vol. 18, p. 241.

secondary revision from the dream-work may have been the fact that secondary revision does not take place in all dreams. Statements to this effect can already be found in his earliest works, for instance, when he says the formation of dreams is also, even though not invariably governed by the demand for a rational and intelligible exterior, i.e. something achieved by secondary revision.[1] Elsewhere, Freud states: 'In addition to condensation, displacement and pictorial arrangement of the psychical material, we are obliged to assign it [the dream-work] yet another activity [i.e. secondary revision], though this is not to be found in operation in *every* dream.'[2] In a much later work, Freud refers to secondary revision as a 'further, somewhat variable, factor'.[3] But it seems important to emphasize that even though Freud, in his later works, was inclined no longer to regard secondary revision as a part of the dream-work proper, his basic point of view and conception of the process and functioning of secondary revision remained unaltered, and all that changed was the descriptive use of the term. This is evident from Freud's passage quoted earlier.[4]

[1] (1900a) *The Interpretation of Dreams*, S.E., Vol. 5, p. 533.
[2] (1901a) *On Dreams*, S.E., Vol. 5, p. 666.
[3] (1933a) *New Introductory Lectures on Psycho-Analysis*, S.E., Vol. 22, p. 21.
[4] cf. reference (4) on page 90.

SYMBOLISM

Symbolism is a term related to the employment of symbols to represent in the conscious mind unconscious mental contents that will not otherwise be allowed to enter consciousness. A symbol in very general terms is something standing as a substitute for something else. Symbolization is a final means of expression of repressed material. It is a special kind of indirect representation which is distinguished from the various other forms of pictorial presentation of thought material such as the simile, metaphor, allusion, etc., though it is related to them all. It 'is a substitutive perceptual replacement expression for something hidden, with which it has evident characteristics in common or is coupled by internal associative connections. Its essence lies in its having two or more meanings'.[1] It lends itself to general use on account of its special suitability for disguising the unconscious and essentially is a primitive form of thinking.[2] We derive our knowledge of symbolization from widely differing sources: from fairy tales and myths, jokes and witticisms, from folklore, i.e. from what we know of the manners and customs, sayings and songs, of different peoples, and from poetic and colloquial usage of language.[3]

Dreams 'make use of any symbolizations which are already present in unconscious thinking, because they fit in better with the requirements of dream-construction on account of their representability and also because as a rule they escape censorship'.[4]

Freud spoke of the symbolic as the fourth relation between 'dream elements and the "genuine" thing behind them'.[5]

Later he goes on to say that

---

[1] Rank and Sachs quoted by Jones, E., 'The Theory of Symbolism' (1916) in *Papers on Psycho-Analysis*, 5th edition, The Williams and Wilkins Company, 1948, p. 96.

[2] ibid.

[3] (1916–17) *Introductory Lectures on Psycho-Analysis*, S.E., Vol. 15, p. 158 f.

[4] (1900a) *The Interpretation of Dreams*, S.E., Vol. 5, p. 349.

[5] (1916–17) *Introductory Lectures on Psycho-Analysis*, S.E., Vol. 15, p. 151.

'even if there were no dream-censorship dreams would still not be easily intelligible to us, for we should still be faced with the task of translating the symbolic language of dreams into that of our waking thought. Thus symbolism is a second and independent factor in the distortion of dreams, alongside of the dream-censorship. It is plausible to suppose, however, that the dream censorship finds it convenient to make use of symbolism, since it leads towards the same end the strangeness and incomprehensibility of dreams.'[1]

The symbolic relation is essentially that of a particular kind of comparison. Dreams use symbolism for particular elements of the latent dream thoughts. This comparison is remarkable in that it is not exposed by the process of free association. Also that the dreamer knows nothing about it but makes use of it unaware, even remaining unaware when it is brought to notice.

'The essence of this symbolic relation is that it is a comparison, though not a comparison of *any* sort. Special limitations seem to be attached to the comparison, but it is hard to say what these are. Not everything with which we can compare an object or a process appears in dreams as a symbol for it. And on the other hand a dream does not symbolize every possible element of the latent dream-thoughts but only certain definite ones. So there are restrictions here in both directions. We must admit, too, that the concept of a symbol cannot at present be sharply delimited: it shades off into such notions as those of a replacement or representation, and even approaches that of an allusion. With a number of symbols the comparison which underlies them is obvious. But again there are other symbols in regard to which we must ask ourselves where we are to look for the common element, the *tertium comparitionis*, of the supposed comparison. On further reflection we may afterwards discover it or it may definitely remain concealed. It is strange, moreover, that if a symbol is a comparison it should not be brought to light by an association, and that the dreamer should not be acquainted with it but should make use of it without knowing about it: more than that, indeed, that the dreamer feels no inclination to acknowledge the comparison even after it has been pointed out to him. You see, then, that a symbolic

[1] ibid., p. 168.

relation is a comparison of a quite special kind, of which we do not as yet clearly grasp the basis, though perhaps we may later arrive at some indication of it.'[1]

It [symbolism] is the method by which a dream which expresses erotic wishes can succeed in appearing innocently non-sexual in its manifest content.[2] It can be viewed as displacement in that it consists in the replacement of an important but objectionable element by one that is indifferent and that appears innocent to the censorship like a very remote allusion to the latent content.[3] The concept symbolized may or may not be conscious but the affect investing the concept is repressed and therefore unconscious. The process is carried out unconsciously, the symbol being taken for reality.[4]

A characteristic of symbolism is that its language knows no grammar. It is an extreme case of language of infinitives and even the active and passive are represented by one and the same image.[5] Symbols may have two or more meanings which will be determined by the associations of the patient, or the symbol may be a condensation of many meanings. The symbol has an independence of individual conditioning factors. The individual cannot invest the symbol with a different meaning from anyone else. He can choose from the various meanings of a symbol. For a different meaning he will have to choose from a variety of symbols.[6]

'Dreams make use of this symbolism for the disguised representation of their latent thoughts.' Many symbols are habitually employed to express the same thing. 'Often enough a symbol has to be interpreted in its proper meaning and not symbolically; ... on other occasions the dreamer may derive from his private memories the power to employ as sexual symbols all kinds of things which are not ordinarily employed as such. If a dreamer has

---

[1] ibid., p. 152 f.

[2] (1901a) *On Dreams*, S.E., Vol. 5, p. 682 f.

[3] (1905c) *Jokes and their Relation to the Unconscious*, S.E., Vol. 8, p. 88 f.

[4] Rank and Sachs quoted by Jones, E., 'The Theory of Symbolism' (1916) in *Papers on Psycho-Analysis*, 5th edition, The Williams and Wilkins Company, 1948, p. 96 f.

[5] (1905c) *Jokes and their Relation to the Unconscious*, S.E., Vol. 8, p. 212.

[6] Rank and Sachs quoted by Jones, E., 'The Theory of Symbolism' (1916) in *Papers on Psycho-Analysis*, 5th edition, The Williams and Wilkins Company, 1948, p. 97.

a choice open to him between a number of symbols, he will decide
in favour of the one which is connected in its subject-matter with
the rest of the material of his thoughts. . . . The presence of symbols in dreams not only facilitates their interpretation but also
makes it more difficult.'[1] Symbolic interpretation is really a 'second
and auxiliary method of dream-interpretation'.[2]

'Symbolism is perhaps the most remarkable chapter of the theory
of dreams. In the first place, since symbols are stable translations,
they realize to some extent the ideal of the ancient as well as of the
popular interpretation of dreams, from which, with our technique,
we had departed widely. They allow us in certain circumstances
to interpret a dream without questioning the dreamer, who indeed
would in any case have nothing to tell us about the symbol. If we
are acquainted with the ordinary dream-symbols, and in addition
with the dreamer's personality, the circumstances in which he
lives and the impressions which preceded the occurrence of the
dream, we are often in a position to interpret a dream straightaway
—to translate it at sight, as it were. A piece of virtuosity of this
kind flatters the dream-interpreter and impresses the dreamer; it
forms an agreeable contrast to the laborious work of questioning
the dreamer. But do not allow yourself to be led astray by this. It
is not our business to perform acts of virtuosity. Interpretation
based on a knowledge of symbols is not a technique which can
replace or compete with the associative one. It forms a supplement
to the latter and yields results which are only of use when introduced into it.'[3]

The dreamer has at his command a symbolic mode of expression
of which he knows nothing. This is as if the housemaid finds
herself in full knowledge of the language of Sanscrit without
knowing it.[4] Freud thought this was to be explained by an unconscious knowledge of phylogenetic or ontogenetic origin. In a
number of cases the element in common between a symbol and
what it represents is obvious. In others it is concealed and the
choice of the symbol seems puzzling. It is the latter that must be
able to throw light upon the ultimate meaning of the symbolic

[1] (1900a) *The Interpretation of Dreams*, S.E., Vol. 5, p. 352 f.
[2] ibid., Vol. 4, p. 241 n.
[3] (1916–17) *Introductory Lectures on Psycho-Analysis*, S.E., Vol. 15, p. 151.
[4] ibid., p. 165.

relation. They indicate that it is of a genetic character. Things that are symbolically connected today were probably linked in pre-historic times by conceptual and linguistic identity. Sperber held the view that primal words applied to sexual things in the beginning but lost this through being applied to other things and activities. The symbolic relation is a relic and a mark of former identity.[1] This partially helps explain why in dreams symbols are almost exclusively sexual ones while in other fields other themes occur.[2] According to Sperber's view, in the past man made work agreeable by treating it as an equivalent of and substitute for sexual activities. In time the word became dissociated from the sexual meaning. This may help explain why weapons and tools stand out as the symbol for the male genital while materials and things worked on stand for female genitalia.[3]

In primitive civilization an 'importance was attached to sexual organs and functions that appear to us absolutely monstrous'.[4]

Though the number of symbols is large, the number of subjects symbolized is not large. In dreams those pertaining to sexual life are the overwhelming majority. Mostly they deal with the human body as a whole, with children, brothers and sisters, birth, death and nakedness. They represent the most primitive ideas and interests imaginable.[5] The male genital appears to have a wide variety of symbols.[6] Freud has studied and given an account of a very large number of the symbols that appear in dreams.[7]

Dream symbolism is a small part of the province of symbolism which applies as well to myths, fairy tales, colloquial speech, songs, poetic fantasy, etc.[8]

It may be mentioned that in this area of symbolism several analysts have made important contributions. Freud referred for example to Stekel in this respect. Freud recognized the importance of symbolism in dreams from the very beginning. 'But it was only

---

[1] (1913j) 'The Claims of Psycho-Analysis to Scientific Interest', S.E., Vol. 13, p. 177.
[2] (1916–17) *Introductory Lectures on Psycho-Analysis*, S.E., Vol. 15, p. 166 f.
[3] Jones, E., 'The Theory of Symbolism' in *Papers on Psycho-Analysis*, 5th edition, The Williams and Wilkins Company, 1948, p. 110.
[4] ibid., p. 104.
[5] (1916–17) *Introductory Lectures on Psycho-Analysis*, S.E., Vol. 15, p. 153.
[6] ibid., pp. 154, 163.
[7] (1900a) *The Interpretation of Dreams*, S.E., Vol. 5, pp. 353–60.
[8] (1916–17) *Introductory Lectures on Psycho-Analysis*, S.E., Vol. 15, p. 166.

by degrees and as my experience increased that I arrived at a full appreciation of its extent and significance and, I did so under the influence of the contributions of Wilhelm Stekel (1911) . . .'[1]

[1] [1925] (1900a) *The Interpretation of Dreams*, S.E., Vol. 5, p. 350.

THE REMEMBERING AND
FORGETTING OF DREAMS

All forgetting and remembering has two aspects in general:

1. The removal of attention cathexis from current thoughts and perceptions so that other thoughts and perceptions can enter consciousness in their turn.[1,2]

The original thoughts and perceptions leave memory traces from which, by later processes of condensation and displacement of cathexes are constructed images (memories of perceptions) and concepts (memories of thoughts). These are together organized into complex memories by associative links with other memories and earlier memories of things and words. The memory-traces themselves persist unchanged and not organized.[3,4]

2. There is the other aspect, relating to the pleasure principle of the inability to recall certain memories to consciousness at will, because their content would in itself cause anxiety or unpleasure or because they are unconsciously associated with other memories which are barred from consciousness for the same reasons.

The application of these aspects to dreams
Both these aspects of remembering and forgetting apply to dreams, i.e.

A. *Remembering Dreams*
1. whatever dream contents are admitted to consciousness form the memories of the dream; only these memories are capable of being recalled to consciousness—the dreaming itself is a new experience and not a memory.
2. whether the dream-contents are remembered on awakening or at any time later on, they must pass the barriers of the endo-

---

[1] (1900a) *The Interpretation of Dreams*, S.E., Vol. 5, p. 616.
[2] ibid., p. 617.
[3] [1904] (1901b) *The Psycho-Pathology of Everyday Life*, S.E., Vol. 6, p. 134 f.
[4] [1907] ibid., p. 274 f.

psychic censorship. If this does not happen, they cannot be remembered.

Sometimes it can only be remembered that there was a dream, while all details of the dream are forgotten; or an apparently whole dream is remembered or some details are remembered while others are forgotten; some details are only vaguely remembered and the dreamer doubts whether these memories are correct. Freud described this as follows:

'It has been objected . . . that we have in fact no knowledge of the dreams that we set out to interpret. . . . In the first place, what we remember . . . has been mutilated by the untrustworthiness of our memory . . . frequently . . . we can remember nothing but a single fragment which is itself recollected with peculiar uncertainty. Secondly, there is every reason to suspect that our memory of dreams is not only fragmentary but positively inaccurate and falsified. On the one hand it may be doubted whether what we dreamt was really as disconnected and hazy as our recollection of it; and on the other hand it may also be doubted whether a dream was really as connected as it is in the account we give of it, whether in attempting to reproduce it we do not fill in what was never there, or what has been forgotten, with new and arbitrarily selected material, whether we do not add embellishments and trimmings and round it off so that there is no possibility of deciding what its original content may have been.'[1]

The reasons for this are indicated in the following quotation:

'It is true that we distort dreams in attempting to reproduce them, here we find at work once more the process which we have described as the secondary (and often ill-conceived) revision of the dream by the agency which carried out normal thinking. But this distortion is itself no more than a part of the revision to which the dream-thoughts are regularly subjected as a result of the dream-censorship' . . . he goes on: 'The only mistake made by previous writers has been in supposing that the modification of the dream in the course of being remembered and put into words is an *arbitrary* one and cannot be further resolved and that it is therefore calculated to give us a misleading picture of the dream. They have underestimated the extent to which psychical events

[1] (1900a) The Interpretation of Dreams, S.E., Vol. 5, p. 512.

are determined. There is nothing arbitrary about them. It can be shown quite generally that if an element is left undetermined by one train of thought, its determination is immediately effected by a second one.'[1]

He pointed to the fact that dreams are remembered sometimes for a lifetime.

'Dreams which occur in the earliest years of childhood and are retained in the memory for dozens of years, often with complete sensory vividness, are almost always of great importance in enabling us to understand the history of the subject's mental development and of his neurosis.'[2]

B. Further Freud indicated that 'the *forgetting* of dreams, too, remains inexplicable unless the power of the psychical censorship is taken into account'.[3] . . . 'the forgetting of dreams is to a great extent a product of resistance'.[4] . . . 'dreams are no more forgotten than other mental acts and can be compared, by no means to their disadvantage, with other mental functions in respect of their retention in the memory'.[5]

'We have seen that waking life shows an unmistakable inclination to forget any dream that has been formed in the course of the night—whether as a whole directly after waking, or bit by bit in the course of the day; and we have recognized that the agent responsible for this forgetting is the mental resistance to the dream which has already done what it could against it during the night . . . *the state of sleep makes the formation of dreams possible because it reduces the power of the endopsychic censorship.*'[6]

Not only do the censorship barriers in waking life work in these ways through inability to recall in part or in whole, or inability to recall with certitude; they have also functioned in the formation of the dream-memories through condensation and displacement so that the dream memories may be distorted organizations of the dream material as originally perceived. Analytic work does not

[1] ibid., p. 514.
[2] [1919] p. 522 f.
[3] ibid., p. 517.
[4] ibid., p. 520.
[5] ibid., p. 521.
[6] ibid., p. 525 f.

seek to reconstruct these dream memories accurately, but to lead from them by associative pathways to the recall of memories linking the latent dream-thoughts, from which the latent dream content may be deduced and interpreted.

Freud emphasized the role of resistance in this:

'It is often possible by means of analysis to restore all that has been lost by the forgetting of the dream's content; at least, in quite a number of cases one can reconstruct from a single remaining fragment not, it is true, the dream—which is in any case a matter of no importance—but all the dream-thoughts . . . it shows that there was no lack of a hostile (i.e. resistant) purpose at work in the forgetting of the dream.'[1]

The fact that the patient remembers different fragments in giving a second account of the dream provides the analyst with important clues.

'This resistance has not been exhausted even by the displacements and substitutions it has brought about; it persists in the form of doubt attaching to the material which has been allowed through. We are especially inclined to misunderstand this doubt since it is careful never to attack the more intense elements of a dream but only the weak and indistinct ones. As we already know, however, a complete reversal of all psychical values takes place between the dream thoughts and the dream. Distortion is only made possible by a withdrawal of psychical value; it habitually expresses itself by that means and is occasionally content to require nothing more.'[2]

[1] ibid., p. 517.
[2] ibid., p. 516.

APPARENT FAILURES OF THE
WISH-FULFILLING FUNCTION
OF DREAMS

*Punishment Dreams, Counter-Wish Dreams, Anxiety-Dreams,
Dreams in the Traumatic Neuroses*

Freud discussed a number of apparent exceptions to the theory
that all dreams are fulfilment of wishes, i.e. dreams in which the
manifest content is distressing or unpleasant: Punishment dreams,
counter-wish dreams, anxiety dreams and dreams in the traumatic
neuroses. He found no difficulty in demonstrating the disguised
wish in punishment dreams and counter-wish dreams. Anxiety
dreams, he evidently thought, required more explanation, but
here, too, he was able to show the presence of an unconscious wish.
At one time he thought that dreams occurring in the traumatic
neuroses might prove the exception to the rule, but he eventually
reached the conclusion that even in these dreams there was an
attempt at the fulfilment of a wish. However, it was the occurrence
of these dreams in the traumatic neuroses that caused him to
modify his formulation from: '*A dream is a (disguised) fulfilment
of a (suppressed or repressed) wish*',[1] to ' . . . a dream is an attempt
at the fulfilment of a wish'.[2]

Punishment-Dreams

In a 1919 addition to *The Interpretation of Dreams* Freud showed
that what is fulfilled in punishment-dreams is a wish that the
dreamer may be punished for his repressed and forbidden wishful
impulses.[3] Thus punishment dreams differ from other wishful
dreams.

'The essential characteristic of punishment-dreams would thus be
that in their case the dream-constructing wish is not an unconscious wish derived from the repressed (from the system un-

[1] (1900a) *The Interpretation of Dreams*, S.E., Vol. 4, p. 160.
[2] (1933a) *New Introductory Lectures on Psycho-Analysis*, S.E., Vol. 22, p. 29.
[3] [1919] (1900a) *The Interpretation of Dreams*, S.E., Vol. 5, p. 557.

THE THEORY OF DREAMS

conscious, but a punitive one reacting against it and belonging to the ego, though at the same time an unconscious (that is to say, preconscious) one.'[1]

'Punishment-dreams, too, are fulfilments of wishes, though not of wishes of the instinctual impulses but of those of the critical, censoring and punishing agency in the mind. If we have a pure punishment dream before us, an easy mental operation will enable us to restore the wishful dream to which the punishment-dream was the correct rejoinder and which, owing to this repudiation, was replaced as the manifest dream.'[2]

Counter-wish Dreams
In a 1909 addition to *The Interpretation of Dreams*[3] Freud noted the existence of dreams which appear to contradict the theory that all dreams are fulfilments of wishes, in that their subject matter is the frustration of a wish. However, this holds only for the manifest content. Interpretation of the dream in the usual way will reveal an underlying wish, namely, a masochistic one, which is gratified by the apparent frustration.

'There is a masochistic component in the sexual constitution of many people, which arises from the reversal of an aggressive, sadistic component into its opposite. Those who find their pleasure, not in having *physical* pain inflicted on them, but in humiliation and mental torture, may be described as 'mental masochists'. It will at once be seen that people of this kind can have counter-wish dreams and unpleasurable dreams, which are none the less wish-fulfilments since they satisfy their masochistic inclinations.'[4] [Note that in later theoretical formulations Freud revised his views on the origin of masochism, considering it rather to be a primary phenomenon.]

Freud noted also that in a large number of 'counter-wish' dreams occuring in his patients while in resistance, he could discern a wish to prove his theory wrong. Many people had a counter-wish dream following their first introduction to his theory.

---

[1] [1919] ibid., p. 558.
[2] (1933a) *New Introductory Lectures on Psycho-Analysis*, S.E., Vol. 22, p. 27 f.
[3] [1909] (1900a) *The Interpretation of Dreams*, S.E., Vol. 4, pp. 157–9.
[4] ibid., p. 159.

The example he gives shows that this [probably preconscious] wish to disprove Freud's theory covered and was reinforced by another, unconscious wish.[1]

Anxiety Dreams

Anxiety dreams, i.e. those dreams which are accompanied by anxiety, leading to the awakening of the dreamer, were discussed at length by Freud since they presented the greatest apparent contradiction to the wish-fulfilment theory. He continued to develop his understanding of them throughout his years of work on dreams. In 1900 he pointed out that in the majority of dreams forbidden unconscious wishes are only able to be represented as fulfilled because they are so distorted and disguised by the dream-work that they are no longer objectionable to the censorship. But in anxiety dreams the dream-work fails to disguise the forbidden wish sufficiently, so the dream fails in its function of making a compromise between the unconscious wish which is seeking fulfilment and the preconscious wish to sleep, which requires the suppression of unconscious excitation.

'The dream-process is allowed to begin as a fulfilment of an unconscious wish; but if this attempted wish fulfilment jars upon the preconscious so violently that it is unable to continue sleeping, then the dream has made a breach in the compromise and has failed to carry out the second half of its task. In that case the dream is immediately broken off and replaced by a state of complete waking ... what I have in mind is of course the case of anxiety-dreams, and in order that I may not be thought to be evading this evidence against the theory of wish-fulfilment whenever I come across it, I will at all events give some hints of their explanation.

'There is no longer anything contradictory to us in the notion that a psychical process which develops anxiety can nevertheless be the fulfilment of a wish. We know that it can be explained by the fact that the wish belongs to one system, the unconscious, while it has been repudiated and suppressed by the other system, the preconscious.'[2]

[1] ibid., p. 157 f.
[2] ibid., Vol. 5, p. 579 f.

This statement belongs to the period of Freud's first anxiety theory, when he considered anxiety to arise from the direct transformation of repressed libido. He regarded anxiety dreams as part of the problem of neurosis, i.e. of anxiety and repression in general. In 1900 he discussed anxiety-dreams as 'a special sub-species of dreams with a distressing content'.[1] (See also 'Affects in Dreams'.)

He there compared anxiety in dreams to that occurring in a phobia, '. . . in both cases the anxiety is only superficially attached to the idea that accompanies it; it originates from another source'. This source, Freud thought was '. . . libido which has been diverted from its purpose and has found no employment'. He concluded that 'anxiety dreams are dreams with a sexual content, the libido belonging to which has been transformed into anxiety'.[2]

Freud considered the use made by the dream-work of somatic sources of anxiety, and distinguished two classes of anxiety dream: those in which anxiety associated with repressed wishes corresponds to repressed libido, and those in which anxiety is associated with a somatic condition of disease, and may be exploited by the dream in expressing forbidden wishes. In the latter case the feeling of anxiety associated with, for example, difficulty in breathing due to disease of the lungs or heart

'. . . is exploited in order to assist the fulfilment in the form of dreams of energetically suppressed wishes which, if they had been dreamt about for *psychical* reasons, would have led to a similar release of anxiety. . . . We can put it that in the first case a somatically determined affect is given a psychical interpretation; while in the other case, though the whole is psychically determined, the content which had been suppressed is easily replaced by a somatic interpretation appropriate to anxiety. The difficulties which all this offers to our understanding have little to do with dreams: they arise from the fact that we are here touching on the problem of the generation of anxiety and on the problem of repression.'[3]

He further says:

'. . . anxiety dreams only occur if the censorship has been wholly or partly overpowered; and, on the other hand, the overpowering

[1] ibid., Vol. 4, p. 160.
[2] ibid., p. 161 f.
[3] ibid., p. 236 f.

of the censorship is facilitated if anxiety has already been produced as an immediate sensation arising from somatic sources. We can thus plainly see the purpose for which the censorship exercises its office and brings about the distortion of dreams: it does so *in order to prevent the generation of anxiety or other forms of distressing affect.*'[1]

In 1916, discussing the fact that the fulfilment of wishes does not bring pleasure to the dreamer, but its opposite—anxiety, Freud observed that,

'anxiety-dreams often have a content entirely devoid of distortion, a content which has, so to speak, evaded the censorship. An anxiety-dream is often the undisguised fulfilment of a wish—not, of course, of an acceptable wish, but of a repudiated one. The generation of anxiety has taken the place of the censorship. Whereas we can say of an infantile dream that it is the open fulfilment of a permitted wish, and of an ordinary distorted dream that it is the disguised fulfilment of a repressed wish, the only formula that fits an anxiety-dream is that it is the open fulfilment of a repressed wish. The anxiety is a sign that the repressed wish has shown itself stronger than the censorship, that it has put through, or is on the point of putting through, its wish-fulfilment in spite of the censorship.'[2]

When Freud revised his theory of anxiety in 1926,[3] he did not specifically reformulate his theory about anxiety dreams. Probably this was because no essential changes were required to the wish-fulfilment theory. The concept of conflict, in topographical terms between an unconscious repressed wish and the preconscious repressing force (the censorship), or in structural terms between an id impulse and the ego, remained unchanged. All that required reformulation was the place of origin of the anxiety experienced by the dreamer. This was no longer seen as derived from the *transformation* of the forbidden unconscious libidinal impulse, but was seen as *arising in the ego, in reaction* to the libidinal impulse which threatens to break through into consciousness. Indeed many of his

[1] ibid., p. 267.
[2] (1916–17) *Introductory Lectures on Psycho-Analysis*, S.E., Vol. 15, pp. 215–17.
[3] (1926d) *Inhibitions, Symptoms and Anxiety*, S.E., Vol. 20.

earlier discussions (e.g. pages 105 and 107) can be equally well understood with either theory in mind.

It seems likely that Freud already had in mind the idea of anxiety as originating in the ego prior to the structural formulations of 1923 and the new anxiety theory of 1926. In a passage added to *The Interpretation of Dreams* in 1919 he says:

'. . . it may happen that the sleeping ego takes a still larger share in the constructing of the dream, that it reacts to the satisfying of the repressed wish with violent indignation and itself puts an end to the dream with an outburst of anxiety.'[1]

Dreams in the Traumatic Neuroses

The only type of dream which gave Freud reason to concede that not all dreams were wish-fulfilments were the dreams occurring in the traumatic neuroses. He discussed these in *Beyond the Pleasure Principle*, together with dreams occurring during analysis which revive traumatic experiences of infancy, and concluded that these dreams, unlike all others, were not under the dominance of the pleasure principle, but were helping to carry out another task, '. . . endeavouring to master the stimulus retrospectively, by developing the anxiety whose omission was the cause of the traumatic neurosis'.

He raised the question of whether wish-fulfilment was not, after all, the primary purpose of dreams, and stated the possibility that their original function may have been the fulfilment of the compulsion to repeat.

'This would seem to be the place, then, at which to admit for the first time an exception to the proposition that dreams are fulfil-ments of wishes. Anxiety dreams, as I have shown repeatedly and in detail, offer no such exception. Nor do "punishment dreams", . . . But it is impossible to classify as wish-fulfilments the dreams we have been discussing which occur in traumatic neuroses, or the dreams during psycho-analyses which bring to memory the psychical traumas of childhood. They arise, rather, in obedience to the compulsion to repeat, though it is true that in analysis that compulsion is supported by the wish (which is encouraged by suggestion) to conjure up what has been forgotten and repressed.

[1] [1919] (1900a) *The Interpretation of Dreams*, S.E., Vol. 5, p. 557.

Thus it would seem that the function of dreams, which consists in setting aside any motives that might interrupt sleep, by ful-filling the wishes of the disturbing impulses, is not their *original* function. It would not be possible for them to perform that function until the whole of mental life had accepted the dominance of the pleasure principle. If there is a "beyond the pleasure principle", it is only consistent to grant that there was also a time before the purpose of dreams was the fulfilment of wishes. This would imply no denial of their later function.'[1]

Again, in 1923, Freud says 'so far as I can at present see, dreams that occur in a traumatic neurosis are the only *genuine* exceptions . . . to the rule that dreams are directed towards wish-fulfilment'.[2] However, by 1933, Freud seemed inclined to reverse this opinion, and to think not that dreams in traumatic neuroses performed a function other than wish-fulfilment, but rather that they were examples of dreams in which the attempt to fulfil a wish had failed. In the *New Introductory Lectures on Psycho-Analysis* he discusses the revival of distressing childhood experiences in dreams during analysis and concludes that, nevertheless, there has been an attempt by the dream-work to turn the memories of the original disappointing, frightening or painful experiences into fulfilments of the instinctual wishes connected with the unpleasant experi-ences.[1] He goes on,

'With the traumatic neuroses things are different. In their case the dreams regularly end in the generation of anxiety. We should not, I think, be afraid to admit that here the function of the dream has failed. I will not invoke the saying that the exception proves the rule: its wisdom seems to me most questionable. But no doubt the exception does not overturn the rule. If, for the sake of studying it, we isolate one particular psychical function, such as dreaming, from the psychical machinery as a whole, we make it possible to discover the laws that are peculiar to it; but when we insert it once more into the general context we must be prepared to discover that these findings are obscured or impaired by collision with other forces. We say that a dream is a fulfilment of a wish; but if

[1] (1920g) *Beyond the Pleasure Principle*, S.E., Vol. 18, p. 32 f.
[2] (1923c) 'Remarks on the Theory and Practice of Dream-Interpretation,' S.E., Vol. 19, p. 118.
[1] (1933a) *New Introductory Lectures on Psycho-Analysis*, S.E., Vol. 22, p. 28 f.

you want to take these latter objections into account, you can say nevertheless that a dream is an *attempt* at the fulfilment of a wish. No one who can properly appreciate the dynamics of the mind will suppose that you have said anything different by this. In certain circumstances a dream is only able to put its intention into effect very incompletely, or must abandon it entirely. Unconscious fixation to a trauma seems to be foremost among obstacles to the function of dreaming. While the dreamer is obliged to dream, because the relaxation of repression at night allows the upward pressure of the traumatic fixation to become active, there is a failure in the functioning of his dream-work, which would like to transform the memory-traces of the traumatic event into the fulfilment of a wish. In these circumstances it will happen that one cannot sleep, that one gives up sleep from dread of the failure of the function of dreaming. Traumatic neuroses are here offering us an extreme case; but we must admit that childhood experiences, too, are of a traumatic nature, and we need not be surprised if comparatively trivial interferences with the function of dreams may arise under other conditions as well.'[1]

Thus it would seem that Freud eventually returned to the view that there are no genuine exceptions to the rule that the function of dreams is to fulfil wishes. The apparent exceptions are only examples of the dream's failure to fulfil its function.

[1] ibid., p. 29 f.

DREAM INTERPRETATION

Dream interpretation is the process whereby the latent meaning is arrived at by starting from the manifest content of the dream. This process essentially requires the patient to free-associate to the elements of the dream (as he remembers it), which includes identifying the day-residues contained in the dream.[1] These associative chains of thought lead to certain central ideas, which may recur more than once.[2] From these central themes, and together with his own knowledge of the patient's psychopathology and dream-symbols, the analyst can then deduce the repressed unconscious wish usually of an infantile sexual nature (and aggressive one at times)[3] which was the motive force of the dream, and which constitutes its latent meaning.[4]

Freud says:

'We need not suppose that every association that occurs during the work of interpretation had a place in the dream-work during the night. It is true that in carrying out the interpretation in the waking state we follow a path which leads back from the elements of the dream to the dream-thoughts, and that the dream-work followed one in the contrary direction. But it is highly improbable that these paths are passable both ways. It appears, rather, that in the daytime we drive shafts which follow along fresh chains of thought and that these shafts make contact with the intermediate thoughts and the dream-thoughts now at one point and now at another. We can see how in this manner fresh daytime material inserts itself into the interpretative chains. It is probable too that the increase in resistance that has set in since the night makes new and more devious detours necessary.'[5]

Of the dream symbolism, Freud says 'it is important for the

---

[1] (1900a) *The Interpretation of Dreams*, S.E., Vols. 4 and 5, pp. 165, 527.
[2] ibid., Vol. 5, p. 640.
[3] ibid., Vol. 4, p. 250 f.
[4] ibid., p. 682.
[5] ibid., Vol. 4, p. 311 and Vol. 5, p. 532.

technique of dream interpretation. With the help of a knowledge of dream symbolism it is possible to understand the meaning of separate elements of the content of a dream . . . without having to ask the dreamer for his associations'. Nevertheless he adds:

'quite apart from the use of individual symbols and oscillations in the use of universal ones, one can never tell whether any particular element in the content of a dream is to be interpreted symbolically or in its proper sense, and one can be certain that the *whole* content of a dream is not to be interpreted symbolically. A knowledge of dream symbolism will however afford the most valuable assistance to interpretation precisely at those points at which the dream's associations are insufficient or fail altogether.'[1]

Furthermore he adds the following warning:

'Regard for scientific criticism forbids our returning to the arbitrary judgement of the dream-interpreter, as it was employed in ancient times and seems to have been revived in the reckless interpretations of Stekel. We are thus obliged, in dealing with those elements of the dream-content which must be recognized as symbolic, to adopt a combined technique, which on the one hand rests on the dreamer's associations and on the other hand fills the gaps from the interpreter's knowledge of symbols. We must combine a critical caution in resolving symbols with a careful study of them in dreams which afford particularly clear instances of their use, in order to disarm any charge of arbitrariness in dream-interpretation.'[2]

The value of dream interpretation is the information which it yields about the unconscious activities of the mind. Freud says,

'The unconscious is the true psychical reality; *in its innermost nature it is as much unknown to us as the reality of the external world, and it is as incompletely presented by the data of consciousness as is the external world by the communications of our sense organs.*'[3] [Dreams] have proved that what is suppressed continues to exist in normal people as well as abnormal, and remains capable of psychical functioning. Dreams themselves are among the

[1] ibid., Vol. 4, p. 245 and Vol. 5, pp. 353 and 683–5.
[2] ibid., Vol. 5, p. 353.
[3] ibid., Vol. 5, p. 613.

manifestations of this suppressed material. . . . '*The interpretation of dreams is the royal road to a knowledge of the unconscious activities of the mind.*'[1]

We have not here been dealing with the specific technique of Dream Interpretation, and those interested in this aspect should refer to p. 626, Vol. 5, the Standard Edition, where there is a list of writings by Freud dealing predominantly or largely with Dreams.

[1] ibid., Vol. 5, p. 608.

DAY-DREAMS (FANTASIES) AND DREAMS

Freud has alluded in very many of his papers to the similarities between day-dreams and dreams. According to him day-dreams share a large number of their properties with night-dreams and their investigation might in fact have served as the shortest and best approach to an understanding of night-dreams.[1] Like dreams they are wish-fulfilments and based to a great extent on impressions of infantile experiences. Like dreams they benefit from a certain degree of relaxation from the censorship, etc.

There are nevertheless basic differences between day-dreams and night-dreams. In dreams 'we attach complete belief to the hallucinations. . . . It is this characteristic that distinguishes true dreams from day-dreaming, which is never confused with reality.'[2]

The day-dream is a form of thinking during waking life that takes place in the conscious or the preconscious and obeys its own laws, having its own peculiarities. The night-dreams have been described by Freud as merely a *'form of thinking'*, a transformation of preconscious material of thought by the dream-work and its condition. It takes place during the sleeping state.[3]

Quite apart from the similarities and differences of these two types of mental phenomena, fantasies can play an important role in dreams which we attempt to describe shortly in what follows.

When considering the role played by fantasies in the formation of dreams we should bear in mind that at times Freud refers to unconscious fantasies in the descriptive sense meaning preconscious fantasies, that is, fantasies that are not presently conscious—though on the other hand they are quite capable of becoming conscious at any point. These preconscious fantasies referred to as unconscious fantasies are not topographically speaking unconscious (in contrast to the repressed unconscious

---

[1] (1900a) *The Interpretation of Dreams*, S.E., Vol. 5, p. 491 f.
[2] ibid., Vol. 4, p. 50.
[3] (1922b) 'Some Neurotic Mechanisms in Jealousy, Paranoia and Homosexuality', S.E., Vol. 18, p. 229.

fantasies). All they need to become conscious is attention cathexis since there is no conflict with them and no force opposing their reaching consciousness. Confusion in these respects is liable to produce a great deal of misunderstanding of the role played by fantasies in the formation of dreams, which can be on the side of the repressed unconscious impulses or as part of the latent dream thoughts (preconscious and conscious components).

Some '*unconscious fantasies*' (topographically speaking) could be the ideational content attached to some impulses that have been repressed. These repressed unconscious impulses may well be the essential element in the construction of a particular dream, the real core of the dream. They will look for expression in consciousness through the association with the available latent-dream thoughts and day residues like in the case of any other repressed unconscious impulse. In this case presumably they have to suffer all the distortions imposed by the censorship before they can gain access to consciousness in addition to the distortion due to considerations of representability, condensation and displacement. What appears then in the manifest content is a derivative of the original fantasy after the dream-work has dealt with the material available for the dream. How far removed from the original fantasy and wish will depend on dynamic, economic, etc., conditions existing at the time of the dream in the mental apparatus. They can vary from one dream to the other and are very much dependent on the state of the ego at any time. (Ego exhausted, etc.)

But the fantasies can be part of the *preconscious and conscious latent dream thoughts* and it will seem that in this case the secondary revision can make use of them or part of them for its purposes of constructing a facade for the dream. (See draft Dream Fantasies.) In the case of *repressed unconscious fantasies* this will not be possible in the same way.

Consequently some dreams will merely consist in the repetition of a daytime fantasy which may perhaps have remained unconscious in the descriptive sense. It happens more frequently though that the ready-made fantasy forms only a portion of a dream, or that only a portion of the fantasy forces its way into the dream.[1]

Thereafter the fantasy is treated in general like any other portion

[1] (1900a) *The Interpretation of Dreams*, S.E., Vol. 5, p. 492 f.

of the latent material, though it often remains recognizable in the dream. Freud pointed to his having avoided giving account of dreams in which unconscious fantasies play any considerable part, because the introduction of unconscious fantasies would have necessitated a long discussion on the psychology of unconscious thinking.[1]

To understand the role of fantasies in dreams it becomes important to consider at which point the *secondary revision* comes into action, and how it makes use of fantasies. (See Dream Fantasies and Secondary Revision.)

[1] (1900a) *The Interpretation of Dreams*, S.E., Vol. 5, p. 512.

INDEX

acting out, 10–11

affects in dreams, 43–7, 69, 106; belong to latent content, 34; and ideational material of latent dream thoughts, *see* ideational; inhibition of, 37, 44–5, 57–8; less modified, 37, 43, 69; and symbols, 95; unpleasant, and censorship, 57

analyst's influence on latent dream-thoughts, 36

anticathexis, 57

anxiety, 28; censorship aimed at preventing, 68; dreams, 22, 33, 59–60, 68–9, 103–8; —, and intense affect, 46; theory of, 106–8

arousing effect of dreams, 90

associations: free, *see* free; superficial, 63

castration complex, 9

cathexis: attention, 99, 115; (-es) displaced in dream, 73, 79, 83; memory existing as visual, 77; of memories of things, 81, 86; of preconscious thoughts, retained in sleep, 19, 31, 38; in sleep, 25, 50, 57; of system perception, 76, 84

censor, 55; overwhelmed by affects, 46

censoring force in ego, 16

censorship, 56–63, 66, 82; of affects, 43–4, 47; and anxiety dreams, 106–7; and displacement, 84, 86; of dream wish, 24, 31, 34, 41, 68–9, 77; endopsychic, 100–1; and forgetting/remembering dreams, 100–2; of memories, 50; and regression in dreams, 75; relaxed/lowered in sleep, 48, 57, 63, 101; and representability, 71, 73; symbols and, 72, 93–5; wishes, 27, 61, 104; *see also* superego

childhood: dream is revival of, 77; memories, 49–50 (*see also* infantile material); psychical traumas of, 108–10

children, dreams of, 21, 24, 55, 69, 107

composite: figures, 82; idea, 86

compression, *see* condensation

compromise formation, 58, 82; dream is, 24–5, 44, 58, 63, 105

compulsion to repeat, 108

condensation, 50, 52, 62–6, 68, 71–3, 76, 79–82, 91–2, 99; displacement and, 83–4, 86–7, 101, 115; symbolism and, 95

conflict, concept of, 107

conscious wishes, 32–3

contradictory characteristics of dream, 81–2

convenience, dreams of, 21, 55

day's residues, 19–22, 24–5, 28–30, 36, 40–2, 49, 111, 115; preconscious, 21, 28, 31, 63, 66, 73; reinforced with instinctual impulses, 38–9, 63–4

defence, 47–8; *see also* censorship

delusions, 16

disease, detected in dreams, 22, 106; *see also* somatic stimuli

displacement, 41, 47, 52, 63, 65–6, 71–3, 79, 83–7, 91–2; of accent, 59; of cathexes, 62, 64, 68, 81, 99; and memories, 49–50, 81; and symbolism, 95

dissolution of complex, 47

distortion: dream-, 58–60, 68–70, 86; of dream wish, 18, 34, 45, 61; of latent thoughts and impulses, 55, 57; of memories, 48–50

dream-work, 15, 18, 23, 26, 29, 33–4, 36–7, 41, 52, 54, 58, 62–7, 83; and affects, 44, 46–7; and anxiety dreams, 105; four activities of, 65, 91–2; *see also* condensation; displacement; plastic representation; secondary revision

ego: anxiety arising in, 107–8; and censor, 56; defences of, 31, 83 ego—*contd.*

(*see also* censorship; displacement);
desire, 22 (*see also* day's residue);
dreams arising from, 41; ideal, 56;
regression, 78; (*see also* regression);
repressive resistance of, 58; wish to
sleep, 22, 26, 57 (*see also* sleep)
energy(-ies): cathectic, 83; transference, 74; *see also* cathexis

façade of dream, 52, 55, 62, 65, 68, 88,
90, 115; *see also* secondary revision
fantasies: based on infantile experiences, 32, 39, 54; and day-dreams,
114–16; dream-, 39, 52–3, 90;
poetic, 97
father-complex, 9
Ferenczi, S., 86
fixation, traumatic, 110
forgetting of dreams, 69–70, 99–102
fragmented form of memories, 50–1
free association, 94, 96, 111
Freud, Sigmund, WORKS: *An Autobiographical Study*, 15n.–16n., 10n.–
21n., 36n., 38n., 58n., 60n.; *Beyond
the Pleasure Principle*, 108; 'The
Claims of Psycho-Analysis to Scientific Interest', 35n., 36n., 97n.;
*Delusions and Dreams in Jensen's
'Gradiva'*, 21n., 36n., 39n.; 'On
Dreams', 15n., 26n., 35n., 37n.,
57n., 63n., 65n., 69n., 79n., 81n.–
82n., 87n., 89n.–90 & n., 92n., 95n.;
'An Evidential Dream', 29n., 35n.,
40n., 91 & n.; 'Five Lectures on
Psycho-Analysis', 36n.; 'From the
History of an Infantile Neurosis',
17n.; *Inhibitions, Symptoms and
Anxiety*, 107n.; *Interpretation of
Dreams*, passim; *Introductory Lectures on Psycho-Analysis*, 15n.–18n.,
54n.–56n., 59n., 68n.–69n., 79 & n.,
82n.–84n., 88n., 93n.–97n., 107n.;
*Jokes and their Relation to the Un-
conscious*, 35n., 36n., 66n., 84n.,
95n.; 'A Metapsychological Supplement to the Theory of Dreams',
17n., 25 & n., 28n., 32n., 34n.,
39n., 57n., 63n.–65n., 73n., 86n.,
88n.; 'A Mythological Parallel to a
Visual Obsession', 16n.; 'On Narcissism: An Introduction', 56n.;
*New Introductory Lectures on Psycho

-Analysis*, 15n., 21n., 26n.–27n.,
30n., 33n.–34n., 40n., 61n., 65n.,
72n., 81n., 85, 86n., 93n., 103n.–
104n., 109 & n.; *An Outline of
Psycho-Analysis*, 21n.; 68n.; *Psychopathology of Everyday Life*, 82n.,
99n.; 'Remarks on the Theory and
Practice of Dream-Interpretation',
36n., 109n.; 'Some Additional
Notes on Dream-Interpretation as a
Whole', 61n.; 'Some Neurotic
Mechanisms in Jealousy, Paranoia
and Homosexuality', 114n.; *Totem
and Taboo*, 37n., 89n.; 'Two
Encyclopaedia Articles', 35n., 36n.,
57n., 68n., 71n., 91n.; 'The Unconscious', 79n., 83n.

guilt-complex, 9

hallucinations in dreams, 18, 57, 75–6,
78, 114
hallucinatory: cathexis of perceptual
systems, 74; representation of
dream-thoughts, 75; revival of
perceptual images, 76; wish-fulfilment, 16, 25, 63–5, 72
hypermnesic dreams, 48, 50

id: dreams arising from, 41, 68;
impulse, 22, 31; *see also* wish, unconscious
ideas of great psychical significance, 80
ideational material of latent dream
thoughts, 37, 43, 115; and affects,
46–7, 85
identifications, 71
images: as memories of perception,
see memories; thoughts transformed
into, *see* visual
'immoral' dreams, 60–1
infantile material/wish in dreams, 20
24, 29, 31–3, 39, 45, 50, 75, 77–8,
111; disguised in manifest contact,
54; fantasies based on, *see* fantasies
inhibition of affect, 37, 44–5
instigators, dream, 19–22, 33, 87;
conscious wish as, 23; day's residues
as, 40 (*see also* day's residues)
instinctual impulses: infantile, 77;
impulse, unconscious/repressed, 30,
32, 38, 41–2; *see also* wish, unconscious

intellectual judgement/operations in dreams, 38, 65

intermediate common entity, 87

interpretation, work of, 28, 111–13; and symbolism, 96–8

jokes, 81, 93

Jones, E.: 'The Theory of Symbolism' 93n., 95n.

language: concrete, rich in associations, 64, 73; poetic and colloquial use of, 93; and symbolism, 95

latent dream content, 15, 28–34, 102; compared with manifest, 79

latent dream thoughts, 19–20, 25, 28–32, 35–9, 52, 55, 58–60, 65, 69, 84, 102, 115; affects in, 34, 43–7; and condensation, 80; descriptively unconscious, 29, 36; distinguished from dream-work, 34; distinguished from manifest content, see manifest; dynamically/topographically preconscious, 29, 36; and representability, 71; and symbolism, 94–5; transformed into manifest content by dream-work, 62, 68, 72 (see also dream-work); see also preconscious dream thoughts

laws of dream-formation, 48, 50

logical relations belonging to dream-thoughts, 74, 76; and secondary revision, 88–92; of similarity, consonance, and common attributes, 81

manifest content of dreams, 54–5, 58; affects in, 34, 43; distinguished from latent, 33, 35–6, 54; memories in, 48; and secondary revision, 90–1

masochistic wish in dreams, 104–5

Maury's guillotine dream, 53

meanings of dream, many, 37

memory(-ies); distorts dreams, 69; existing as visual cathexes, 77; of perceptions/images, 99; revived, 20, 32; of thoughts/concepts, 99; -traces, 33, 40, 64, 78, 99, 110; —, stored in mnemonic systems, 75; —, visual or acoustic, 62; unconscious, 75–6; used in dreams, 48–51; visual, in unconscious, 80

mnemic images, 76, 78

mnemic/mnemonical systems, 19, 74–6

mother-complex, 9

myths, 93, 97

narcissistic state of sleep, 17, 22, 57

neurosis(-es), 24, 40–1; traumatic, 108–10

neurotic symptom(s), 77; dreams as, 16, 58

obsessions, 16

Oedipus complex, 9

opposite: affects turned into, 37; thought yoked with its, 44–5

overdetermination, 45, 85; of affects, 46; of single image or word, 72

perception: backward course to, 80; images as memories of, 99; thought becomes conscious as, 63–5, 77

perception/perceptual system, 75–6, 80–1

phobia, 106

phylogenetic origin of unconscious knowledge, 96

pictorial character of manifest content, 36, 62, 64, 84, 92–3; see also hallucinations; visual images

pictures, thoughts transformed into, 80

plastic representation, 65, 71–4; see also representability

pleasure principle, 99, 109

preconscious: contents and unconscious mutual influence of, 48; days' residues, see day's residues; dream thoughts, 23, 32, 35–6; (see also latent dream thoughts); material, 29, 34; quiescent force of, 90; system, 19, 31, 56; wishes, 26; wish to sleep, 26

primary process, 79, 81, 83, 86; laws of, 68; phenomena, 50, 64; and secondary revision, 91; see also condensation; displacement

psychosis(-es): dreams as transient, 16; hallucinatory wishful, 63, 78

punishment dreams, 27, 61, 103–4

Rank, Otto, 93n., 95n.

real and imaginary events, 39

wish–*contd.*

repressed, 22, 27, 32, 34, 38, 61; to sleep, *see* sleep; unconscious, 23–4, 26, 38; —, controlled by censor, 56–7 (*see also* censor); —, in dynamic sense, 29, 31–2; —, as motive force of dream, 40; *see also* id impulse

wish-fulfilment, dreams as, 17, 21–3, 31, 33, 38, 42, 44, 63; —, disguised, 58; —, undisguised, 21, 55, 69; failures of, 103–10; hallucinatory, 16, 25

word: cathexes, 75; in dreams, 82

word/verbal presentations, 73, 82, 86; *see also* verbal ideas

words, primal, applied to sexual things 97